FIRST AS TRAGEDY,
THEN AS FARCE

FIRST AS TRAGEDY, THEN AS FARCE

◆

SLAVOJ ŽIŽEK

VERSO
London • New York

First published by Verso 2009
© Slavoj Žižek 2009
All rights reserved

5 7 9 10 8 6

Verso
UK: 6 Meard Street, London W1F 0EG
US: 20 Jay Street, Suite 1010, Brooklyn, NY 11201
www.versobooks.com

Verso is the imprint of New Left Books

ISBN-13: 978-1-84467-428-2

British Library Cataloguing in Publication Data
A catalogue record for this book is available from the British Library

Library of Congress Cataloging-in-Publication Data
A catalog record for this book is available from the Library of Congress

Typeset by Hewer Text UK Ltd, Edinburgh

Printed in the UK by CPI Bookmarque, Croydon

Contents

Introduction:
The Lessons of the First Decade

The title of this book is intended as an elementary IQ test for the reader: if the first association it generates is the vulgar anti-communist cliché—"You are right—today, after the tragedy of twentieth-century totalitarianism, all the talk about a return to communism can only be farcical!"—then I sincerely advise you to stop here. Indeed, the book should be forcibly confiscated from you, since it deals with an entirely different tragedy and farce, namely, the two events which mark the beginning and the end of the first decade of the twenty-first century: the attacks of September 11, 2001 and the financial meltdown of 2008.

We should note the similarity of President Bush's language in his addresses to the American people after 9/11 and after the financial collapse: they sounded very much like two versions of the same speech. Both times Bush evoked the threat to the American way of life and the need to take fast and decisive action to cope with the danger. Both times he called for the partial suspension of American values (guarantees of individual freedom, market capitalism) in order to save these very same values. From whence comes this similarity?

Marx began his *Eighteenth Brumaire* with a correction of Hegel's idea that history necessarily repeats itself: "Hegel remarks somewhere that all great events and characters of world history occur, so to speak, twice. He forgot to add: the first time as tragedy, the second time as farce."[1] This

---

1 Karl Marx, "The Eighteenth Brumaire of Louis Bonaparte," in *Surveys From Exile*, edited and introduced by David Fernbach, Harmondsworth: Penguin 1973, p. 146.

supplement to Hegel's notion of historical repetition was a rhetorical figure which had already haunted Marx years earlier: we find it in his "A Contribution to the Critique of Hegel's Philosophy of Right," where he diagnoses the decay of the German *ancien régime* in the 1830s and 1840s as a farcical repetition of the tragic fall of the French *ancien régime*:

> It is instructive for [the modern nations] to see the *ancien régime*, which in their countries has experienced its *tragedy*, play its *comic* role as a German phantom. Its history was *tragic* as long as it was the pre-existing power in the world and freedom a personal whim—in a word, as long as it believed, and had to believe, in its own privileges. As long as the *ancien régime*, as an established world order, was struggling against a world that was only just emerging, there was a world-historical error on its side but not a personal one. Its downfall was therefore tragic.
>
> The present German regime, on the other hand—an anachronism, a flagrant contradiction of universally accepted axioms, the futility of the *ancien régime* displayed for all the world to see—only imagines that it still believes in itself and asks the world to share in its fantasy. If it believed in its own *nature*, would it try to hide that nature under the *appearance* of an alien nature and seek its salvation in hypocrisy and sophism? The modern *ancien régime* is rather merely the *clown* of a world order whose *real heroes* are dead. History is thorough and passes through many stages while bearing an ancient form to its grave. The last phase of a world-historical form is its *comedy*. The Greek gods, who already died once of their wounds in Aeschylus's tragedy *Prometheus Bound*, were forced to die a second death—this time a comic one—in Lucian's *Dialogues*. Why does history take this course? So that mankind may part *happily* with its past. We lay claim to this *happy* historical destiny for the political powers of Germany.[2]

---

2   Karl Marx, "A Contribution to the Critique of Hegel's Philosophy of Right," in *Early Writings*, introduced by Lucio Colletti, Harmondsworth: Penguin 1975, pp. 247–8.

Note the precise characterization of the German *ancien régime* as the one which "only imagines that it still believes in itself"—one can even speculate about the meaning of the fact that, during the same period, Kierkegaard deployed his idea that we humans cannot ever be sure that we believe: ultimately, we only "believe that we believe." The formula of a régime which "only imagines that it believes in itself" nicely captures the cancellation of the performative power ("symbolic efficiency") of the ruling ideology: it no longer effectively functions as the fundamental structure of the social bond. And, we may ask, are we not today in the same situation? Do today's preachers and practitioners of liberal democracy not also "only imagine that they believe in themselves," in their pronunciations? In fact, it would be more appropriate to describe contemporary cynicism as representing an exact inversion of Marx's formula: today, we only imagine that we do *not* "really believe" in our ideology—in spite of this imaginary distance, we continue to practise it. We believe not less but much more than we imagine we believe. Benjamin was thus indeed prescient in his remark that "everything depends on how one believes in one's belief."[3]

Twelve years prior to 9/11, on November 9, 1989, the Berlin Wall fell. This event seemed to announce the beginning of the "happy '90s," Francis Fukuyama's utopia of the "end of history," the belief that liberal democracy had, in principle, won out, that the advent of a global liberal community was hovering just around the corner, and that the obstacles to this Hollywood-style ending were merely empirical and contingent (local pockets of resistance whose leaders had not yet grasped that their time was up). September 11, in contrast, symbolized the end of the Clintonite period, and heralded an era in which new walls were seen emerging everywhere: between Israel and the West Bank, around the European Union, along the US–Mexico border, but also within nation-states themselves.

---

3 Walter Benjamin, *Gesammelte Briefe*, Vol. I, Frankfurt: Suhrkamp Verlag 1995, p. 182.

In an article for *Newsweek*, Emily Flynn Vencat and Ginanne Brownell report how today,

> the members-only phenomenon is exploding into a whole way of life, encompassing everything from private banking conditions to invitation-only health clinics ... those with money are increasingly locking their entire lives behind closed doors. Rather than attend media-heavy events, they arrange private concerts, fashion shows and art exhibitions in their own homes. They shop after-hours, and have their neighbors (and potential friends) vetted for class and cash.

A new global class is thus emerging "with, say, an Indian passport, a castle in Scotland, a *pied-à-terre* in Manhattan and a private Caribbean island"—the paradox is that the members of this global class "dine privately, shop privately, view art privately, everything is private, private, private." They are thus creating a life-world of their own to solve their anguishing hermeneutic problem; as Todd Millay puts it: "wealthy families can't just 'invite people over and expect them to understand what it's like to have $300 million.'" So what *are* their contacts with the world at large? They come in two forms: business and humanitarianism (protecting the environment, fighting against diseases, supporting the arts, etc.). These global citizens live their lives mostly in pristine nature—whether trekking in Patagonia or swimming in the translucent waters of their private islands. One cannot help but note that one feature basic to the attitude of these gated superrich is *fear*: fear of external social life itself. The highest priorities of the "ultrahigh-net-worth individuals" are thus how to minimize security risks—diseases, exposure to threats of violent crime, and so forth.[4]

In contemporary China, the new rich have built secluded communities modeled upon idealized "typical" Western towns; there is, for example, near Shanghai a "real" replica of a small English town,

---

4   Emily Flynn Vencat and Ginanne Brownell, "Ah, the secluded life," *Newsweek*, December 10, 2007.

including a main street with pubs, an Anglican church, a Sainsbury supermarket, etc.—the whole area is isolated from its surroundings by an invisible, but no less real, cupola. There is no longer a hierarchy of social groups within the same nation—residents in this town live in a universe for which, within its ideological imaginary, the "lower class" surrounding world simply *does not exist*. Are not these "global citizens" living in secluded areas the true counter-pole to those living in slums and other "white spots" of the public sphere? They are, indeed, two sides of the same coin, the two extremes of the new class division. The city that best embodies that division is São Paulo in Lula's Brazil, which boasts 250 heliports in its central downtown area. To insulate themselves from the dangers of mingling with ordinary people, the rich of São Paulo prefer to use helicopters, so that, looking around the skyline of the city, one really does feel as if one is in a futuristic megalopolis of the kind pictured in films such as *Blade Runner* or *The Fifth Element*, with ordinary people swarming through the dangerous streets down below, whilst the rich float around on a higher level, up in the air.

It thus seems that Fukuyama's utopia of the 1990s had to die twice, since the collapse of the liberal-democratic political utopia on 9/11 did not affect the economic utopia of global market capitalism; if the 2008 financial meltdown has a historical meaning then, it is as a sign of the end of the economic face of Fukuyama's dream. Which brings us back to Marx's paraphrase of Hegel: one should recall that, in his introduction to a new edition of *Eighteenth Brumaire* in the 1960s, Herbert Marcuse added yet another turn of the screw: sometimes, the repetition in the guise of a farce can be more terrifying than the original tragedy.

This book takes the ongoing crisis as a starting point, gradually moving to "related matters," by way of unraveling its conditions and implications. The first chapter offers a diagnosis of our predicament, outlining the utopian core of the capitalist ideology which determined both the crisis itself and our perceptions of and reactions to it. The second chapter endeavors to locate aspects of our situation which open up the space for new forms of communist praxis.

What the book offers is not a neutral analysis but an engaged and extremely "partial" one—for *truth is partial*, accessible only when one takes sides, and is no less universal for this reason. The side taken here is, of course, that of communism. Adorno begins his *Three Studies on Hegel* with a rebuttal of the traditional question about Hegel exemplified by the title of Benedetto Croce's book *What Is Living and What Is Dead in the Philosophy of Hegel?* Such a question presupposes, on the part of the author, the adoption of an arrogant position as judge of the past; but when we are dealing with a truly great philosopher the real question to be raised concerns not what this philosopher may still tell us, what he may still mean to us, but rather the opposite, namely, what *we* are, what our contemporary situation might be, in *his* eyes, how our epoch would appear to *his* thought. And the same should apply to communism—instead of asking the obvious question "Is the idea of communism still pertinent today, can it still be used as a tool of analysis and political practise?" one should ask the opposite question: "How does our predicament today look from the perspective of the communist idea?" Therein resides the dialectic of the Old and the New: it is those who propose the constant creation of new terms ("postmodern society," "risk society," "informational society," "postindustrial society," etc.) in order to grasp what is going on today who miss the contours of what is actually New. The only way to grasp the true novelty of the New is to analyze the world through the lenses of what was "eternal" in the Old. If communism really is an "eternal" Idea, then it works as a Hegelian "concrete universality": it is eternal not in the sense of a series of abstract-universal features that may be applied everywhere, but in the sense that it has to be re-invented in each new historical situation.

In the good old days of Really Existing Socialism, a joke popular among dissidents was used to illustrate the futility of their protests. In the fifteenth century, when Russia was occupied by Mongols, a peasant and his wife were walking along a dusty country road; a Mongol warrior on a horse stopped at their side and told the peasant he would now proceed to rape his wife; he then added: "But since there is a lot of dust on the ground, you must hold my testicles while I rape your wife, so that they will not get dirty!" Once the Mongol had done the deed and ridden away, the peasant started laughing and jumping with joy. His surprised wife asked: "How can you be jumping with joy when I was just brutally raped in your presence?" The farmer answered: "But I got him! His balls are covered with dust!" This sad joke reveals the predicament of the dissidents: they thought they were dealing serious blows to the party *nomenklatura*, but all they were doing was slightly soiling the *nomenklatura*'s testicles, while the ruling elite carried on raping the people . . .

Is today's critical Left not in a similar position? (Among the contemporary names for ever-so-slightly smearing those in power, we could list "deconstruction," or the "protection of individual freedoms.") In a famous confrontation at the university of Salamanca in 1936, Miguel de Unamuno quipped at the Francoists: "*Venceréis, pero no convenceréis*" ("You will win, but you will not convince")—is this all that today's Left can say to triumphant global capitalism? Is the Left predestined to continue to play the role of those who, on the contrary, convince but nevertheless still lose (and are especially convincing in retroactively explaining the reasons for their own failure)? Our task is to discover how to go a step further. Our Thesis 11 should be: in our societies, critical Leftists have hitherto only succeeded in soiling those in power, whereas the real point is to castrate them . . .

But how can we do this? We should learn here from the failures of twentieth century Leftist politics. The task is not to conduct the castration in a direct climactic confrontation, but to undermine those in power with patient ideologico-critical work, so that although they are still in power, one all of a sudden notices that the powers-that-be are afflicted with unnaturally high-pitched voices. Back in the 1960s, Lacan named the irregular short-lived periodical of his school *Scilicet*—the message was not the word's predominant meaning today ("namely," "to wit," "that is to say"), but literally "it is permitted to know." (To know what?—what the Freudian School of Paris thinks about the unconscious . . .) Today, our message should be the same: it is permitted to know and to fully engage in communism, to again act in full fidelity to the communist Idea. Liberal permissiveness is of the order of *videlicet*—it is permitted to *see*, but the very fascination with the obscenity we are allowed to observe prevents us from *knowing what it is that we see*.

The moral of the story: the time for liberal-democratic moralistic blackmail is over. Our side no longer has to go on apologizing; while the other side had better start soon.

1   It's Ideology, Stupid!

Capitalist Socialism?

The only truly surprising thing about the 2008 financial meltdown is how easily the idea was accepted that its happening was an unpredictable surprise which hit the markets out of the blue. Recall the demonstrations which, throughout the first decade of the new millennium, regularly accompanied meetings of the IMF and the World Bank: the protesters' complaints took in not only the usual anti-globalizing motifs (the growing exploitation of Third World countries, and so forth), but also how the banks were creating the illusion of growth by playing with fictional money, and how this would all have to end in a crash. It was not only economists such as Paul Krugman and Joseph Stiglitz who warned of the dangers ahead and made it clear that those who promised continuous growth did not really understand what was going on under their noses. In Washington in 2004, so many people demonstrated about the danger of a financial collapse that the police had to mobilize 8,000 additional local policemen and bring in a further 6,000 from Maryland and Virginia. What ensued was tear-gassing, clubbing and mass arrests—so many that police had to use buses for transport. The message was loud and clear, and the police were used literally to stifle the truth.

After this sustained effort of wilful ignorance, it is no wonder that, when the crisis did finally break out, as one of the participants put it, "No one really [knew] what to do." The reason being that expectations are part of the game: how the market will react depends not only on how much people trust this or that intervention, but even more so on how much they think *others* will trust them—one cannot take into account the effects of one's own choices. Long ago, John Maynard Keynes rendered this self-referentiality nicely when he compared the stock market to a silly competition in which the participants have to pick several pretty girls from a hundred photographs, the winner being the one who chooses girls closest to the average opinion: "It is not a case of choosing those which, to the best of one's judgment, are really the prettiest, nor even those which average opinion genuinely thinks the prettiest. We have reached the third degree where we devote our intelligence to anticipating what average opinion expects the average opinion to be."[1] So, we are forced to choose without having at our disposal the knowledge that would enable a qualified choice, or, as John Gray put it: "*We are forced to live as if we were free.*"[2]

At the height of the meltdown, Joseph Stiglitz wrote that, in spite of the growing consensus among economists that any bail-out based on US Treasury Secretary Henry Paulson's plan would not work,

it is impossible for politicians to do nothing in such a crisis. So we may have to pray that an agreement crafted with the toxic mix of special interests, misguided economics, and right-wing ideologies that produced the crisis can somehow produce a rescue plan that works—or whose failure doesn't do too much damage.[3]

He is correct, since markets are effectively based on beliefs (even beliefs about other people's beliefs), so when the media worry about "how the markets will react" to the bail-out, it is a question not only about its real

---

1   John Maynard Keynes, *The General Theory of Employment, Interest and Money*, New York: Management Laboratory Press 2009, Chapter 12.

2   John Gray, *Straw Dogs*, New York: Farrar Straus and Giroux 2007, p. 110.

3   Joseph Stiglitz, "The Bush administration may rescue Wall Street, but what about the economy?" *The Guardian*, September 30, 2008.

consequences, but about the *belief* of the markets in the plan's efficacy. This is why the bail-out may work even if it is economically wrong-headed.[4]

The pressure "to do something" here is like the superstitious compulsion to make some gesture when we are observing a process over which we have no real influence. Are not our acts often such gestures? The old saying "Don't just talk, do something!" is one of the most stupid things one can say, even measured by the low standards of common sense. Perhaps, rather, the problem lately has been that we have been doing too much, such as intervening in nature, destroying the environment, and so forth. . . Perhaps it is time to step back, think and *say* the right thing. True, we often talk about something instead of doing it; but sometimes we also do things in order to avoid talking and thinking about them. Such as throwing $700 billion at a problem instead of reflecting on how it arose in the first place.

In the ongoing confusion, there is certainly sufficient material to cause us to think things through. Back on July 15, 2008, Republican Senator Jim Bunning attacked Fed Chairman Ben Bernanke, claiming that his proposal showed how "socialism is alive and well in America": "Now the Fed wants to be the systemic risk regulator. But the Fed is the systemic risk. Giving the Fed more power is like giving the neighborhood kid who broke your window playing baseball in the street a bigger bat and thinking that will fix the problem."[5] On September 23, he struck again, calling the Treasury's plan for the biggest financial bail-out since the Great Depression "un-American":

Someone must take those losses. We can either let the people who made bad decisions bear the consequences of their actions, or we can spread that pain to others. And that is exactly what the Secretary proposes

---

4   Since, however, we are repeatedly told that trust and belief are crucial, we should also ask to what extent the Administration's own panicky raising of the stakes itself produced the very danger it was trying to combat.

5   See Edward Harrison, "Senator Bunning blasts Bernanke at Senate hearing," available online at http://www.creditwritedowns.com.

to do—take Wall Street's pain and spread it to the taxpayers. . . . This massive bailout is not the solution, it is financial socialism, and it is un-American.

Bunning was the first to publicly outline the contours of the reasoning behind the Republican Party revolt against the bail-out plan, which climaxed in the rejection of the Fed's proposal on September 29. The argument deserves a closer look. Note how Republican resistance to the bail-out project was formulated in "class warfare" terms: Wall Street versus Main Street. Why should we help those on "Wall Street" responsible for the crisis, while asking ordinary mortgage-holders on "Main Street" to pay the price? Is this not a clear case of what economic theory calls "moral hazard," defined as "the risk that somebody will behave immorally because insurance, the law, or some other agency will protect them against any loss that his or her behavior might cause"—if I am insured against fire, say, I will take fewer fire precautions (or, in extremis, even set fire to my fully insured but loss-generating premises)? The same goes for the big banks: are they not protected against big losses and able to keep their profits? No wonder that Michael Moore wrote a letter to the public decrying the bail-out plan as the robbery of the century.

It is this unexpected overlapping of the views of the Left with those of conservative Republicans which should give us pause for thought. What the two perspectives share is their contempt for the big speculators and corporate managers who profit from risky decisions but are protected from failures by "golden parachutes." Recall the cruel joke from Lubitsch's *To Be or Not to Be*: when asked about the German concentration camps in occupied Poland, the responsible Nazi officer "concentration camp Erhardt" snaps back: "We do the concentrating, and the Poles do the camping." Does the same not hold for the Enron bankruptcy scandal of January 2002, which can be interpreted as a kind of ironic commentary on the notion of the risk society? Thousands of employees who lost their jobs and savings were certainly exposed to risk, but without having had any real choice in the matter—the risk appeared to them as blind fate. On the contrary, those who did have some insight into the risks involved, as well as the power to intervene in the situation (namely, the top managers), minimized their risks by cashing in their stocks and options before the bankruptcy. It is indeed true that we live in a society of risky choices, but it is one in which only some do the choosing, while others do the risking . . .

Is the bail-out plan really a "socialist" measure then, the birth of state socialism in the US? If it is, it is a very peculiar form: a "socialist" measure whose primary aim is not to help the poor, but the rich, not those who borrow, but those who lend. In a supreme irony, "socializing" the banking system is acceptable when it serves to save capitalism. Socialism is bad— except when it serves to stabilize capitalism. (Note the symmetry with China today: in the same way, the Chinese Communists use capitalism to enforce their "Socialist" regime.)

But what if "moral hazard" is inscribed into the very structure of capitalism? That is to say, *there is no way to separate the two*: in the capitalist system, welfare on Main Street depends on a thriving Wall Street. So, while Republican populists who resist the bail-out are doing the wrong thing for the right reasons, the proponents of the bail-out are doing the right thing for the wrong reasons. To put it in more sophisticated terms, the relationship is non-transitive: while what is good for Wall Street is not necessarily good for Main Street, Main Street cannot thrive if Wall Street is feeling sickly, and this asymmetry gives an a priori advantage to Wall Street.

Recall the standard "trickle-down" argument against egalitarian redistribution (through high levels of progressive taxation, etc.): instead of making the poor richer, it makes the rich poorer. Far from being simply anti-interventionist, this attitude actually displays a very accurate grasp of economic state intervention: although we all want the poor to become richer, it is counter productive to help them directly, since they are not the dynamic and productive element in society. The only kind of intervention needed is that which helps the rich get richer;

the profits will then automatically, by themselves, diffuse amongst the poor . . . Today, this takes the form of the belief that if we throw enough money at Wall Street it will eventually trickle down to Main Street, helping ordinary workers and homeowners. So, again, if you want people to have money to build homes, don't give it to them directly, but to those who will in turn lend them the cash. According to the logic, this is the only way to create genuine prosperity; otherwise, it will just be a case of the state distributing funds to the needy at the expense of the real wealth-creators.

Consequently, those who preach the need for a return from financial speculation to the "real economy" of producing goods to satisfy real people's needs, miss the very point of capitalism: self-propelling and self-augmenting financial circulation is its only dimension of the Real, in contrast to the reality of production. This ambiguity was made clear in the recent meltdown when we were simultaneously bombarded by calls for a return to the "real economy" and by reminders that financial circulation, a sound financial system, is the lifeblood of our economies. What strange lifeblood is this which is not part of the "real economy"? Is the "real economy" in itself like a bloodless corpse? The populist slogan "Save Main Street, not Wall Street!" is thus totally misleading, a form of ideology at its purest: it overlooks the fact that what keeps Main Street going under capitalism *is* Wall Street! Tear *that* Wall down and Main Street will be flooded with panic and inflation. Guy Sorman, an exemplary ideologist of contemporary capitalism, is thus indeed correct when he claims: "There is no economic rationale for distinguishing 'virtual capitalism' from 'real capitalism': nothing real has ever been produced without first being financed . . . even in a time of financial crisis, the global benefits of the new financial markets have surpassed their costs."[6]

While financial meltdowns and crises are obvious reminders that

---

6 Guy Sorman, "Behold, our familiar cast of characters," *The Wall Street Journal* (Europe), July 20–1, 2001.

the circulation of Capital is not a closed loop which can fully sustain itself—that it presupposes an absent reality where actual goods that satisfy people's needs are produced and sold—their more subtle lesson is that there can be no return to this reality, *pace* all the rhetoric of "let us return from the virtual space of financial speculation to real people who produce and consume." The paradox of capitalism is that you cannot throw out the dirty water of financial speculation while keeping the healthy baby of real economy.

It is all too easy to dismiss this line of reasoning as a hypocritical defense of the rich. The problem is that, insofar as we remain in a capitalist order, *there is a truth within it*: namely, that kicking at Wall Street really *will* hit ordinary workers. This is why the Democrats who supported the bail-out were not being inconsistent with their Leftist leanings. They would have been inconsistent only if they had accepted the premise of the Republican populists: that (true, authentic) capitalism and the free market economy are a popular, working-class affair, while state intervention is an upper-class elite strategy designed to exploit hard-working ordinary folks. "Capitalism versus socialism" thus becomes ordinary hard-working people versus the upper-class strata.

But there is nothing new with regard to strong state intervention in the banking system or in the economy in general. The recent meltdown itself is a result of such intervention: when, in 2001, the dotcom bubble (which expressed the very essence of the problem of "intellectual property") burst, it was decided to make credit easier in order to redirect growth into housing. (The ultimate cause of the 2008 meltdown was thus, from this point of view, the deadlock of intellectual property.) And, if we broaden our horizon to encompass global reality, we see that political decisions are weaved into the very texture of international economic relations. A couple of years ago, a CNN report on Mali described the reality of the international "free market." The two pillars of Mali economy are cotton in the south and cattle in the north, and both are in trouble because of the way Western powers violate the very rules they try to impose on impoverished Third World nations. Mali produces cotton of top quality, but the problem is that the financial support the US government gives to its own cotton farmers amounts to more than the entire state budget of Mali, so it is no surprise they cannot compete. In the north, the culprit is the European Union: Malian beef cannot compete with heavily subsidized European milk and beef. The EU subsidizes every single cow with around 500 Euros per year—more than the per capita GDP in Mali. As the Malian minister for the economy put it: we don't need your help or advice or lectures on the beneficial effects of abolishing excessive state regulation; please, just stick to your own rules about the free market and our troubles will basically be over ... So where are the Republican defenders of the free market here? The collapse of Mali demonstrates the reality of what it means for the US to put "country first."

What all this clearly indicates is that there is no such thing as a neutral market: in every particular situation, market configurations are always regulated by political decisions. The true dilemma is thus not "Should the state intervene?" but "What kind of state intervention is necessary?" And this is matter for real politics: namely, the struggle to define the basic "apolitical" coordinates of our lives. All political issues are in a way non-partisan; they concern the question: "What *is* our country?" So the debate about the bail-out is precisely *true* politics, to the extent that it deals with decisions about the fundamental features of our social and economic life, and even, in the process, mobilizes the ghosts of class struggle. There is no "objective," expert position simply waiting to be applied here; one just has to take one side or the other, politically.

There is a real possibility that the main victim of the ongoing crisis will not be capitalism but the Left itself, insofar as its inability to offer a viable global alternative was again made visible to everyone. It was the Left which was effectively caught out. It is as if recent events were staged with a calculated risk in order to demonstrate that, even at a time of shattering crisis, there is no viable alternative to capitalism. "Thamzing" is a Tibetan word from the time of Cultural Revolution, with ominous reverberations for liberals: it means a "struggle session," a collective public hearing and criticism of an individual who is aggressively questioned in order to bring about his political re-education through the confession of his or her mistakes and sustained self-criticism. Perhaps today's Left needs one long "thamzing" session?

Immanuel Kant countered the conservative motto "Don't think, obey!" not with the injunction "Don't obey, think!" but rather "Obey, but think!" When we are transfixed by events such as the bail-out plan, we should bear in mind that since this is actually a form of blackmail we must resist the populist temptation to act out our anger and thus wound ourselves. Instead of such impotent acting-out, we should control our fury and transform it into an icy determination to think— to think things through in a really radical way, and to ask what kind of a society it is that renders such blackmail possible.

Crisis As Shock Therapy

Will the financial meltdown be a sobering moment, then, the awakening from a dream? It all depends on how it comes to be symbolized, on what ideological interpretation or story imposes itself and determines the general perception of the crisis. When the normal run of things is traumatically interrupted, the field is then opened up for a "discursive" ideological competition—as happened, for example, in Germany in the early 1930s, when, invoking the Jewish conspiracy, Hitler triumphed in the competition over which narrative best explained the causes for the crisis of the Weimar Republic and offered the best way to escape from that crisis. Likewise, in France in 1940 it was Marshal Pétain's narrative which won out in the struggle to explain the reasons for France's defeat. Any naive Leftist expectation that the current financial and economic crisis necessarily opens up a space for the radical Left is thus without doubt dangerously short-sighted. The primary immediate effect of the crisis will not be the rise of a radical emancipatory politics, but rather the rise of racist populism, further wars, increased poverty in the poorest Third World countries, and greater divisions between the rich and the poor within all societies.

While crises do shake people out of their complacency, forcing them to question the fundamentals of their lives, the most spontaneous first reaction is panic, which leads to a "return to the basics": the basic premises of the ruling ideology, far from being put into doubt, are even more violently reasserted. The danger is thus that the ongoing melt-down will be used in a similar fashion to what Naomi Klein has called the "shock doctrine." There is, indeed, something surprising about the predominantly hostile reactions to Klein's recent book: they are much more violent than one would expect; even benevolent left liberals who sympathize with some of her analyses deplore how "her ranting obscures her reasoning" (as Will Hutton put it in his review of the book in the *Observer*). Clearly, Klein has touched some very sensitive nerves with her key thesis:

> The history of the contemporary free market was written in shocks. Some of the most infamous human rights violations of the past thirty-five years, which have tended to be viewed as sadistic acts carried out by anti-democratic regimes, were in fact either committed with the deliberate intent of terrorizing the public or actively harnessed to prepare the ground for the introduction of radical free-market reforms.7

This thesis is developed through a series of concrete analyses, central among them that of the Iraq War: the US attack on Iraq was sustained by the idea that, following the "shock and awe" military strategy, the country could be organized as a free market paradise, its people being so traumatized that they would offer no opposition. . . The imposition of a full market economy is thus rendered much easier if the way to it is paved by some kind of trauma (natural, military, economic) which, as it were, forces people into shaking off their "old habits," turning them

---

7   Naomi Klein, *The Shock Doctrine: The Rise of Disaster Capitalism*, London: Penguin Books 2007, p. iii.

into an ideological *tabula rasa*, survivors of their own symbolic death, ready to accept the new order now that all obstacles have been swept away. And one can be sure that Klein's shock doctrine holds also for ecological issues: far from endangering capitalism, a widespread environmental catastrophe may well reinvigorate it, opening up new and hitherto unheard-of spaces for capitalist investment.

Perhaps then the economic meltdown will also be used as a "shock," creating the ideological conditions for further liberal therapy? The need for such shock-therapy arises from the (often neglected) *utopian* core of neoliberal economics. The way the market fundamentalists react to the destructive results of implementing their recipes is typical of utopian "totalitarians": they blame all failure on the compromises of those who realized their schemes (there was still too much state intervention, etc.), and demand nothing less than an even more radical implementation of their doctrines.

Consequently, to put it in old-fashioned Marxist terms, the central task of the ruling ideology in the present crisis is to impose a narrative which will place the blame for the meltdown not on the global capitalist system *as such*, but on secondary and contingent deviations (overly lax legal regulations, the corruption of big financial institutions, and so on). Likewise, in the era of Really Existing Socialism, pro-socialist ideologists tried to save the idea of socialism by claiming that the failure of the "people's democracies" was the failure of a non-authentic version of socialism, not of the idea as such, so that existing socialist regimes required radical reforms rather than overthrow and abolition. It is not without irony to note how ideologists who once mocked this critical defense of socialism as illusory, and insisted that one should lay the blame on the very idea itself, now widely resort to the same line of defense: for it is not capitalism as such which is bankrupt, only its distorted realization. . .

Against this tendency, one should insist on the key question: what is the "flaw" in the system *as such* that opens up the possibility for such crises and collapses? The first thing to bear in mind here is that the origin of the crisis is a "benevolent" one: as we have noted, after the dotcom bubble burst, the decision, taken in a bipartisan fashion, was to facilitate real estate investment in order to keep the economy going and prevent recession—today's meltdown is thus simply the price being paid for the measures taken in the US to avoid recession a few years ago. The danger is thus that the predominant narrative of the meltdown will be the one which, instead of awakening us from a dream, will enable us to *continue dreaming*. And it is here that we should start to worry—not only about the economic consequences of the meltdown, but about the obvious temptation to reinvigorate the "war on terror" and US interventionism in order to keep the motor of the economy running, or at least to use the crisis to impose further tough measures of "structural adjustment."

An exemplary case of the way the economic collapse is already being used in the ideologico-political struggle concerns the conflict over what to do with General Motors—should the state allow its bankruptcy or not? Since GM is one of those institutions which embodies the American dream, its bankruptcy was long considered unthinkable. An increasing number of voices, however, now refer to the meltdown as providing that additional nudge which should make us accept the unthinkable. A *New York Times* column entitled "Imagining a G.M. Bankruptcy" begins ominously with: "As General Motors struggles to avoid running out of cash next year, the once-unthinkable prospect of a G.M. bankruptcy filing is looking a lot more, well, thinkable."[8] After a series of predictable arguments (the bankruptcy would not mean automatic job losses, just a restructuring which would make the company leaner and meaner, better adapted to the harsh conditions of today's economy, and so on and so forth) the column dots the 'i's towards the end, when it focuses on the standoff "between G.M. and its unionized workers and retirees": "Bankruptcy would allow G.M. to *unilaterally reject its collective bargaining agreements*, as long as a judge approved." In other words, bankruptcy should be used to break the backbone of one of the last strong unions in

---

8   "Imagining a G.M. bankruptcy," *New York Times*, December 2, 2008 ("DealBook" in the Business section).

the United States, leaving thousands with lower wages and thousands of others with lower retirement incomes. Note again the contrast with the urgent need to save the big banks: in the case of GM, where the survival of tens of thousands of active and retired workers is at stake, there is, of course, no emergency, but, on the contrary, an opportunity to allow the free market to operate with brutal force. As if the unions, rather than failures of managerial strategy, were to be blamed for GM's troubles! This is how the impossible becomes possible: what was hitherto considered unthinkable within the horizon of the established standards of decent working conditions now becomes acceptable.

In his *Poverty of Philosophy*, Marx wrote that bourgeois ideology loves to historicize: every social, religious, and cultural form is historical, contingent, relative—every form except its own. There *was* history once, but now there is no longer any history:

> Economists have a singular method of procedure. There are only two kinds of institutions for them, artificial and natural. The institutions of feudalism are artificial institutions, those of the bourgeoisie are natural institutions. In this, they resemble the theologians, who likewise establish two kinds of religion. Every religion which is not theirs is an invention of men, while their own is an emanation from God. When the economists say that present-day relations—the relations of bourgeois production— are natural, they imply that these are the relations in which wealth is created and productive forces developed in conformity with the laws of nature. These relations therefore are themselves natural laws independent of the influence of time. They are eternal laws which must always govern society. Thus, there has been history, but there is no longer any. There has been history, since there were the institutions of feudalism, and in these institutions of feudalism we find quite different relations of production from those of bourgeois society, which the economists try to pass off as natural and, as such, eternal.[9]

---

9 Karl Marx, *The Poverty of Philosophy*, Chapter 2, "Seventh and last observation,"

Replace "feudalism" with "socialism" and exactly the same holds true of today's apologists for liberal-democratic capitalism.

No wonder the debate about the limits of liberal ideology is thriving in France—the reason is not the long statist tradition which distrusts liberalism; it is rather that the French distance towards the Anglo-Saxon mainstream enables not only a critical stance, but also a clearer perception of the basic ideological structure of liberalism. If one is looking for a clinically pure, laboratory-distilled version of contemporary capitalist ideology, one need only turn to Guy Sorman. The very title of an interview he recently gave in Argentina—"This Crisis Will Be Short Enough"[10]—signals that Sorman fulfils the basic demand liberal ideology has to satisfy with regard to the financial meltdown, namely, to renormalize the situation: "things may appear harsh, but the crisis will be short, it is just part of the normal cycle of creative destruction through which capitalism progresses." Or, as Sorman himself put it in another of his texts, "creative destruction is the engine of economic growth": "This ceaseless replacement of the old with the new—driven by technical innovation and entrepreneurialism, itself encouraged by good economic policies—brings prosperity, though those displaced by the process, who find their jobs made redundant, can understand-

---

Moscow, Progress Publishers 1955.

And do we not find echoes of the same position in today's discursive "anti-essentialist" historicism (from Ernesto Laclau to Judith Butler), which views every social-ideological entity as the product of a contingent discursive struggle for hegemony? As it was already noted by Fredric Jameson, universalized historicism has a strange ahistorical flavor: once we fully accept and practise the radical contingency of our identities, all authentic historical tension somehow evaporates in the endless performative games of an eternal present. There is a nice self-referential irony at work here: there is history only insofar as there persist remainders of "ahistorical" essentialism. This is why radical anti-essentialists have to deploy all their hermeneutic-deconstructive skills to detect hidden tracés of "essentialism" in what appears to be a postmodern "risk society" of contingencies—were they to admit that we already live in an "anti-essentialist" society, they would have to confront the truly difficult question of the historical character of today's predominant radical historicism itself, i.e., confront the topic of this historicism as the ideological form of "postmodern" global capitalism.

10   "Esta crisis sera bastante breve," interview with a Guy Sorman, *Perfil* (Buenos Aires), November 2, 2008, pp. 38–43.

ably object to it."[11] (This renormalization, of course, co-exists with its opposite: the panic raised by the authorities in order to create a shock among the wider public—"the very fundamentals of our way of life are threatened!"—thereby preparing them to accept the proposed, obviously unjust, solution as inevitable.) Sorman's premise is that, over the last few decades (more precisely, since the fall of socialism in 1990), economics finally became a fully tested science: in an almost laboratory situation, the same country was split into two (West and East Germany, South and North Korea), with each part submitted to an opposing economic system, with unambiguous results.

But is economics really a science? While Sorman admits that the market is full of irrational behavior and reactions, his prescription is—not even psychology, but—"neuroeconomics":

> economic actors tend to behave both rationally and irrationally. Laboratory work has demonstrated that one part of our brain bears blame for many of our economically mistaken short-term decisions, while another is responsible for decisions that make economic sense, usually taking a longer view. Just as the state protects us from Akerlof's asymmetry by forbidding insider trading, should it also protect us from our own irrational impulses?

Of course, Sorman is quick to add that

> it would be preposterous to use behavioral economics to justify restoring excessive state regulations. After all, the state is no more rational than the individual, and its actions can have enormously destructive consequences. Neuroeconomics should encourage us to make markets more transparent, not more regulated.

---

11   This and all remaining quotes in this section are from Guy Sorman, "Economics does not lie," *City Journal*, Summer 2008, available online at http://www.city-journal.org.

With this happy twin-rule of economic science supplemented by neuroeconomics, gone is the epoch of ideological dreams masked as science—as in Marx, whose work "can be described as a materialist rewriting of the Bible. With all persons present there, with the proletariat in the role of Messiah. The ideological thought of the nineteenth century is without debate a materialized theology." But even if Marxism is dead, the naked emperor continues to haunt us in new clothes, chief among them ecologism:

> No ordinary rioters, the Greens are the priests of a new religion that puts nature above humankind. The ecology movement is not a nice peace-and-love lobby but a revolutionary force. Like many a modern day religion, its designated evils are ostensibly decried on the basis of scientific knowledge: global warming, species extinction, loss of biodiversity, superweeds. In fact, all these threats are figments of the Green imagination. Greens borrow their vocabulary from science without availing themselves of its rationality. Their method is not new; Marx and Engels also pretended to root their world vision in the science of their time, Darwinism.

Sorman therefore accepts the claim of his friend José María Aznar that the ecological movement is the "Communism of the twenty-first century":

> It is certain that ecologism is a recreation of Communism, the actual [form of] anticapitalism. . . . However, its other half is composed of a quarter of pagan utopia, of the cult of nature, which is much earlier than Marxism, which is why ecologism is so strong in Germany with its naturalist and pagan tradition. Ecologism is thus an anti-Christian movement: nature has precedence over man. The last quarter is rational, there are true problems for which there are technical solutions.

Note the term "technical solution": rational problems have technical solutions. (Again, a blatantly erroneous claim: confronting ecological problems requires making choices and decisions—about what to produce, what to consume, on what energy to rely—which ultimately concern the very way of life of a people; as such, they are not only not technical, but are eminently political in the most radical sense of involving fundamental social choices.) No wonder, then, that capitalism itself is presented in technical terms, not even as a science but simply as something that works: it needs no ideological justification, because its success is itself sufficient justification. In this regard, capitalism "is the opposite of socialism, which has a manual": "Capitalism is a system which has no philosophical pretensions, which is not in search of happiness. The only thing it says is: 'Well, this functions.' And if people want to live better, it is preferable to use this mechanism, because it functions. The only criterion is efficiency."

This anti-ideological description is, of course, patently false: the very notion of capitalism as a neutral social mechanism is ideology (even utopian ideology) at its purest. The moment of truth in this description is nonetheless that, as Alain Badiou has put it, capitalism is effectively not a civilization of its own, with a specific way of rendering life meaningful. Capitalism is the first socio-economic order which *de-totalizes meaning*: it is not global at the level of meaning (there is no global "capitalist world view," no "capitalist civilization" proper; the fundamental lesson of globalization is precisely that capitalism can accommodate itself to all civilizations, from Christian to Hindu and Buddhist). Capitalism's global dimension can be formulated only at the level of truth-without-meaning, as the "Real" of the global market mechanism. The problem here is not, as Sorman claims, that reality is always imperfect, and that people always need to entertain dreams of impossible perfection. The problem is one of meaning, and it is here that religion is now reinventing its role, rediscovering its mission of guaranteeing a meaningful life to those who participate in the meaningless functioning of the capitalist machine. This is why Sorman's description of the fundamental difficulty of capitalist ideology is so misplaced:

> From the intellectual and political standpoint, the great difficulty in administering a capitalist system is that it does not give rise to dreams: no one descends to the street to manifest in its favor. It is an economy which changed completely the human condition, which has saved humanity from misery, but no one is ready to convert himself into a martyr of this system. We should learn to deal with this paradox of a system which nobody wants, and which nobody wants because it doesn't give rise to love, which is not enchanting, not a seducer.

This description is, again, patently untrue: if there was ever a system which enchanted its subjects with dreams (of freedom, of how your success depends on yourself, of the run of luck which is just around the corner, of unconstrained pleasures. . .), then it is capitalism. The true problem lies elsewhere: namely; how to keep people's faith in capitalism alive when the inexorable reality of a crisis has brutally crushed such dreams? Here enters the need for a "mature" realistic pragmatism: one should heroically resist dreams of perfection and happiness and accept bitter capitalist reality as the best (or the least bad) of all possible worlds. A compromise is necessary here, a combination of fighting illusory utopian expectations and giving people enough security to accept the system. Sorman is thus no market-liberal fundamentalist or extremist; he proudly mentions that some orthodox followers of Milton Friedman accused him of being a communist because of his (moderate) support of the welfare state:

> There is no contradiction between State and economic liberalism; on the contrary, there is a complex alliance between the two. I think that the liberal society needs a welfare state, first, with regard to intellectual legitimacy—people will accept the capitalist adventure if there is an indispensable minimum of social security. Above this, on a more

mechanic level, if one wants the destructive creativity of capitalism to function, one has to administer it.

Rarely was the function of ideology described in clearer terms—to defend the existing system against any serious critique, legitimizing it as a direct expression of human nature:

An essential task of democratic governments and opinion makers when confronting economic cycles and political pressure is to secure and protect the system that has served humanity so well, and not to change it for the worse on the pretext of its imperfection. . . . Still, this lesson is doubtless one of the hardest to translate into language that public opinion will accept. The best of all possible economic systems is indeed imperfect. Whatever the truths uncovered by economic science, the free market is finally only the reflection of human nature, itself hardly perfectible.

The Structure of Enemy Propaganda

Such ideological legitimization also perfectly exemplifies Badiou's precise formula of the basic paradox of enemy propaganda: it fights something regarding which it is itself unaware, something to which it is structurally blind—not the actual counter-forces (political opponents), but the *possibility* (the utopian revolutionary-emancipatory potential) which is immanent to the situation:

The goal of all enemy propaganda is not to annihilate an existing force (this function is generally left to police forces), but rather to annihilate an *unnoticed possibility of the situation*. This possibility is also unnoticed by those who conduct this propaganda, since its features are to be simultaneously immanent to the situation and not to appear in it.[12]

---

12 Alain Badiou, Seminar on Plato at the ENS, February 13, 2008 (unpublished).

This is why enemy propaganda against radical emancipatory politics is by definition cynical—not in the simple sense of not believing its own words, but at a much more basic level: it is cynical precisely insofar as it *does* believe its own words, since its message is a resigned conviction that the world we live in, even if not the best of all possible worlds, is the least bad, such that any radical change will only make things worse. (As always with effective propaganda, this normalization can easily be combined with its opposite, reading the economic crisis in religious terms—Benedict XVI, always sharp when it comes to opportunistic maneuvering, was expeditious in capitalizing on the financial crisis along these lines: "This proves that all is vanity, and that only the word of God holds!") There should thus be no surprise that the financial meltdown of 2008 also propelled Jacques-Alain Miller to intervene in such a "constructive" way, to prevent panic:

The monetary signifier is one of semblance, which rests on social conventions. The financial universe is an architecture made of fictions and its keystone is what Lacan called a "subject supposed to know", to know why and how. Who plays this part? The concert of authorities, from where sometimes a voice is detached, Alan Greenspan, for example, in his time. The financial players base their behavior on this. The fictional and hyper-reflexive unit holds by the "belief" in the authorities, i.e. through the transference to the subject supposed to know. If this subject falters, there is a crisis, a falling apart of the foundations, which of course involves effects of panic. However, the financial subject supposed to know was already quite subdued because of deregulation. And this happened because the financial world believed itself, in its infatuated delusion, to be able to work things out without the function of the subject supposed to know. Firstly, the real state assets become waste. Secondly, gradually shit permeates everything. Thirdly, there is a gigantic negative transfer vis-à-vis the authorities; the electric shock of the Paulson/Bernanke plan angers the public: the crisis is one of trust; and it will last till the subject supposed to know is reconstructed.

This will come in the long term by way of a new set of Bretton Woods accords, a council enjoined to speak the truth about the truth.[13]

Miller's reference point here is Alan Greenspan, *the* non-partisan "subject supposed to know" of the long period of economic growth from the Reagan era till the recent debacle. When, on October 23, 2008, Greenspan was submitted to a congressional hearing, he conceded some interesting points in answering his critics who claimed that he had encouraged the bubble in housing prices by keeping interest rates too low for too long, and that he had failed to rein in the explosive growth of risky and often fraudulent mortgage lending.[14] Here is the climactic moment of the hearing, as Representative Henry A. Waxman of California, Chairman of the Oversight Committee, intervened:

I'm going to interrupt you. The question I have for you is, you had an ideology. This is your statement. "I do have an ideology. My judgment is that free competitive markets are by far the unrivalled way to organize economies. We have tried regulation, none meaningfully worked." That was your quote. You had the authority to prevent irresponsible lending practices that led to the subprime[15] mortgage crisis. You were advised to do so by many others. And now our whole economy is paying its price. Do you feel that your ideology pushed you to make decisions that you wish you had not made?[16]

---

13   Jacques-Alain Miller, "The financial crisis," available online at http://www.lacan.com.

14   See Elizabeth Olson, "Greenspan under fire," available online at http://*www.portfolio.com*.

15   A term coined by the media during the credit crunch of 2007 to refer to financial institutions which provide credit to borrowers deemed "subprime" (sometimes also referred to as "under-banked"), i.e., those with a heightened perceived risk of default, such as those who have a history of loan delinquency, those with a recorded bankruptcy, or those with limited debt experience.

16   See Online NewsHour, October 23, 2008, Transcript, "Greenspan admits 'flaw' to Congress, predicts more economic problems," available online at http://www.pbs.org/newshour.

Greenspan answered: "I found a flaw in the model that I perceived as the critical functioning structure that defines how the world works." In other words, Greenspan conceded that, when a "once-in-a-century credit tsunami" engulfed the financial markets, his free market ideology of shunning regulation was proven flawed. Later, Greenspan reiterated his "shocked disbelief" that financial companies had failed to maintain sufficient "surveillance" of their trading counterparties to prevent surging losses: "Those of us who have looked to the self-interest of lending institutions to protect shareholders' equity, myself included, are in a state of shocked disbelief."

This last statement reveals more than may appear at first glance: it indicates that Greenspan's mistake was to expect that the lending institutions' enlightened self-interest would make them act more responsibly, more ethically, in order to avoid short-term self-propelling cycles of wild speculation which, sooner or later, burst like a bubble. In other words, his mistake concerned not the facts, the objective economic data or mechanisms; it concerned rather the ethical attitudes generated by market speculation—in particular the premise that market processes will spontaneously generate responsibility and trust, since it is in the long-term self-interest of the participants themselves to act thusly. Clearly, Greenspan's error was not only and not simply one of overestimating the rationality of market agents—that is, their ability to resist the temptation of making wild speculative gains. What he forgot to include in the equation was the financial speculators' quite rational expectation that the risks would be worth taking, since, in the event of a financial collapse, they could count on the state to cover their losses.

Parenthetically, one of the weird consequences of the financial meltdown and the measures taken to counteract it was a revival of interest in the work of Ayn Rand, the closest one can get to an ideologist of the "greed is good" form of radical capitalism. The sales of Rand's magnum opus, *Atlas Shrugged*, exploded again. One suggested reason for this success was that the Obama administration's support for beleaguered banks smacks of tyrannical socialism, forcing the strong and successful to prop up the weak, feckless and incompetent. "The current economic strategy is right out of *Atlas Shrugged*," the commentator Stephen Moore wrote recently in *Wall Street Journal*. "The more incompetent you are in business, the more handouts the politicians will bestow on you."[17]

According to some reports, there are already signs that the scenario described in *Atlas Shrugged*—of creative capitalists themselves going on strike—is actually coming about. According to John Campbell, a Republican congressman: "The achievers are going on strike. I'm seeing, at a small level, a kind of protest from the people who create jobs . . . who are pulling back from their ambitions because they see how they'll be punished for them."[18] The absurdity of this reaction lies in the fact that it totally misreads the situation: most of the bail-out money is going in gigantic sums to precisely those Randian deregulated "titans" who failed in their "creative" schemes and thereby brought about the downward spiral. It is not the great creative geniuses who are now helping out lazy ordinary people, it is rather the ordinary taxpayers who are helping out the failed "creative geniuses." One need simply recall that the ideologico-political father of the long economic process which resulted in the meltdown is the aforementioned Alan Greenspan, a card-carrying Randian "objectivist."

But let us return to Miller, for the message of his weird text is clear: let us wait patiently for the new "subject supposed to know" to emerge. Miller's position here is one of pure liberal cynicism: we all know that the "subject supposed to know" is a transferential illusion—but we know this "in private," as psychoanalysts. In public, we should promote the rise of the new "subject supposed to know" in order to control panic reactions . . .

Miller has recently been engaged in a struggle against the Europe-wide attempt to impose state regulation of psychoanalysis, which

17   Oliver Burkeman, "Look out for number one," *Guardian*, March 10, 2009, p. 3.
18   Ibid.

would effectively lead to its absorption into the vast field of "scientific" cognitivist and bio-chemical therapies. Unfortunately, he inscribes this struggle in terms of the Right-liberal insistence on the freedom of individuals from socialist and paternalist state control and regulation, referring directly to the work of the pro-Thatcherite neoliberal, Willem H. Buiter.[19] What Miller ignores is how the very state regulations he so ferociously opposes are enacted on behalf of the protection of individuals' autonomy and freedom: he is thus fighting the consequences of the very ideology on which he relies. The paradox is that, in today's digitalized society where not only the state but also big companies are able to penetrate and control individual lives to an unheard-of extent, state regulation is needed in order to maintain the very autonomy it is supposed to endanger.

In the middle of April 2009, I was sitting in a hotel room in Syracuse, hopping between two TV programs: a documentary on Pete Seeger, the great American folk singer of the Left, and a Fox News report on the anti-tax "tea party" in Austin, Texas, with a country singer performing an anti-Obama song full of complaints about how Washington is taxing hard-working ordinary people in order to finance the rich Wall Street financiers. The short-circuit between the two programs had an electrifying effect on me, with two especially noticeable features. First, there was the weird similarity between the two musicians, both formulating a populist anti-establishment critique of the exploitative rich and their state, and both calling for radical measures, up to and including civil disobedience—another painful remainder that, with regard to forms of organization, the contemporary radical-populist Right strangely reminds us of the old radical-populist Left. Second, one cannot but notice the fundamental irrationality of the "tea party" protests: Obama effectively plans to *lower* taxes for over 95 percent of hard-working ordinary people, proposing to raise them for only the upper couple of percentiles—

---

19   See Willem H. Buiter, "Le nouveau Paternalisme: attention, danger!" *Le Nouvel Ane*, September 9, 2008, p. 34–5.

that is, for the "exploitative rich." So how is it that people are literally acting counter to their own interests?

Thomas Frank aptly described this paradox of contemporary populist conservatism in the US:[20] the economic class opposition (poor farmers and blue-collar workers versus lawyers, bankers, and large companies) is transposed or re-coded onto the opposition of honest, hard-working Christian Americans versus the decadent liberals who drink *lattes* and drive foreign cars, advocate abortion and homosexuality, and mock patriotic sacrifice and simple "provincial" ways of life, and so forth. The enemy is thus perceived as the "liberal" elite who, through federal state intervention—from school-busing to legislating that Darwinian theory and perverted sexual practises be taught in class—want to undermine the authentic American way. The conservatives' main economic demand is therefore to get rid of the strong state which taxes the population to finance its regulatory interventions; their minimal economic program is thus: "fewer taxes, fewer regulations." From the standard perspective of the enlightened and rational pursuit of self-interest, the inconsistency of this ideological stance is obvious: the populist conservatives are literally *voting themselves into economic ruin*. Less taxation and deregulation means more freedom for the big companies who are driving impoverished farmers out of business; less state intervention means less federal help for small businessmen and entrepreneurs.

Although the "ruling class" disagrees with the populists' moral agenda, it tolerates the "moral war" as a means of keeping the lower classes in check, that is, it enables the latter to articulate their fury without disturbing the economic status quo. What this means is that the *culture war is a class war* in displaced mode—*pace* those who claim that we live in a post-class society . . . This, however, only makes the enigma even more impenetrable: how is this displacement *possible*? "Stupidity" and "ideological manipulation" are not adequate answers; that is to say, it is

---

20   See Thomas Frank, *What's the Matter with Kansas? How Conservatives Won the Heart of America*, New York: Metropolitan Books 2004.

clearly not good enough to claim that the primitive lower classes have been so brainwashed by the ideological apparatus that they are not or are no longer able to identify their true interests. If nothing else, one should recall how, decades ago, the same state of Kansas identified in Frank's book as a conservative stronghold was once a hotbed of *progressive* populism in the US—and people have certainly not been getting more stupid over the last few decades. Proof of the material force of ideology abounds; in the European elections of June 2009, voters massively supported neoconservative-liberal politics—the very politics that brought about the ongoing crisis. Indeed, who needs direct repression when one can convince the chicken to walk freely into the slaughterhouse?

Sorman's version of capitalist ideology ignores this process of necessary self-blinding and is, as such, too brutal and blatant to be endorsed as hegemonic—it has something of the character of "over-identification" about it, of stating so openly the underlying premises that it becomes embarrassing to all concerned. Rather, the ideological version of capitalism which *is* emerging as hegemonic out of the present crises is that of a "socially responsible" eco-capitalism. While admitting that, in the past and in the present, the free market system has often been over-exploitative with catastrophic consequences, the claim is now made that one can discern the signs of a new orientation which is aware that the capitalist mobilization of a society's productive capacity can also be made to serve ecological goals, the struggle against poverty, and other worthy ends. As a rule, this version is presented as part of a wider shift towards a new holistic post-materialist spiritual paradigm. With the growing awareness of the unity of all life on earth and of the common dangers we all face, a new approach is emerging which no longer opposes the market to social responsibility—they can be reunited for mutual benefit. Collaboration with and the participation of employees, dialogue with customers, respect for the environment, transparency of business deals, are nowadays the keys to success. Capitalists should not just be machines for generating profits, since their lives can have a deeper meaning. Their preferred mottos have become social responsibility and gratitude: they are the first to admit that society has been incredibly good to them by allowing them to deploy their talents and amass great wealth, so it is their duty to give something back to society and to help ordinary people. Only this kind of caring approach makes business success worthwhile ... The new ethos of global responsibility is thus able to put capitalism to work as the most efficient instrument of the common good. The basic ideological *dispositif* of capitalism—we can call it "instrumental reason," "technological exploitation," "individualist greed," or whatever we like—is separated from its concrete socio-economic conditions (capitalist relations of production) and conceived of as an autonomous life or "existential" attitude which should (and can) be overcome by a new more "spiritual" outlook, *leaving these very capitalist relations intact.*

Nevertheless, was the financial meltdown of 2008 not a kind of ironic comment on the ideological nature of this dream of a spiritualized and socially responsible eco-capitalism? As we all know, on December 11, 2008 Bernard Madoff, a highly successful investment manager and philanthropist from Wall Street, was arrested and charged with allegedly running a $50 billion Ponzi (or pyramid) scheme.

On the surface, Madoff's funds were supposed to be low-risk investments. His largest fund reported steady returns, usually gaining a percentage point or two a month. The funds' stated strategy was to buy large cap stocks and supplement those investments with related stock-option strategies. The combined investments were supposed to generate stable returns and also cap losses.

But sometime in 2005, according to the SEC suit, Madoff's investment-advisory business morphed into a Ponzi scheme, taking new money from investors to pay off existing clients who wanted to cash out. ... Despite his gains, a growing number of investors began asking Madoff for their money back. In the first week of December, according to the SEC suit, Madoff told a senior executive that there had been requests from clients for $7 billion in redemptions. ...

Madoff met with his two sons to tell them the advisory business was a fraud—"a giant Ponzi scheme," he reportedly told them—and was nearly bankrupt.[21]

There are two features that make this story so surprising: first, that such a basically simple and well-known strategy was able to succeed in today's allegedly highly complex and controlled field of financial speculation; second, that Madoff was not a marginal eccentric, but a figure from the very heart of the US financial establishment (Nasdaq), involved in numerous charitable activities. One should thus resist the numerous attempts to pathologize Madoff, presenting him as a corrupt scoundrel, a rotten worm in the healthy green apple. Is it not rather that the Madoff case presents us with an extreme but therefore pure example of what caused the financial breakdown itself?

Here one has to ask a naive question: did Madoff not know that, in the long term, his scheme was bound to collapse? What force denied him this obvious insight? Not Madoff's own personal vice or irrationality, but rather a pressure, an inner drive to go on, to expand the sphere of circulation in order to keep the machinery running, inscribed into the very system of capitalist relations. In other words, the temptation to "morph" legitimate business into a pyramid scheme is part of the very nature of the capitalist circulation process. There is no exact point at which the Rubicon was crossed and the legitimate business morphed into an illegal scheme; the very dynamic of capitalism blurs the frontier between "legitimate" investment and "wild" speculation, because capitalist investment is, at its very core, a risky wager that a scheme will turn out to be profitable, an act of borrowing from the future. A sudden uncontrollable shift in circumstances can ruin a supposedly "safe" investment—this is what capitalist "risk" turns on. And, in "postmodern" capitalism, potentially

---

21 Stephen Gandel, "Wall Street's latest downfall: Madoff charged with fraud," *Time*, December 12, 2008.

ruinous speculation is raised to a much higher level than was even imaginable in earlier periods.[22]

Over the last several months, public figures from the Pope downwards have bombarded us with injunctions to fight against the culture of excessive greed and consumption. This disgusting spectacle of cheap moralization is an ideological operation if there ever was one: the compulsion (to expand) inscribed into the system itself is translated into a matter of personal sin, a private psychological propensity. The self-propelling circulation of Capital thus remains more than ever the ultimate Real of our lives, a beast that by definition cannot be controlled, since it itself controls our activity, blinding us to even the most obvious dangers we are courting. It is one big fetishistic denial: "I know very well the risks I am courting, even the inevitability of the final collapse, but nonetheless . . . [I can put off the collapse a little bit longer, take on a little bit more risk, and so on indefinitely]." It is a self-blinding "irrationality" strictly correlative to the "irrationality" of the lower classes voting against their own interests, and yet another proof of the material power of ideology. Like love, ideology is blind, even if the people caught up in it are not.

Human, All Too Human . . .

The contemporary era constantly proclaims itself as post-ideological, but this denial of ideology only provides the ultimate proof that we are more than ever embedded in ideology. Ideology is always a field of struggle—among other things, the struggle for appropriating past traditions. One of the clearest indications of our predicament is the liberal appropriation of Martin Luther King, in itself an exemplary ideological operation. Henry Louis Taylor recently remarked: "Everyone

---

22   Incidentally, it is a sign of the maturity of the US public that there have been no traces of anti-Semitism in their reaction to the financial crisis, although it would have been easy to imagine a reaction such as: "Did you notice how Jews, Jewish financiers, made us hard-working Americans pay $700 billion to cover the costs of their follies!"

knows, even the smallest kid knows about Martin Luther King, can say his most famous moment was that 'I have a dream' speech. No one can go further than one sentence. All we know is that this guy had a dream. We don't know what that dream was."[23] King had come a long way from the crowds who cheered him on at the 1963 March on Washington, when he was introduced as "the moral leader of our nation." By pursuing issues beyond simply that of segregation, he had lost much public support, and was increasingly considered a pariah. As Harvard Sitkoff put it, "he took on issues of poverty and militarism because he considered them vital 'to make equality something real and not just racial brotherhood but equality in fact.'" To put it in Badiou's terms, King followed the "axiom of equality" well beyond the single topic of racial segregation: he was campaigning on anti-poverty and anti-war issues at the time of his death. He had spoken out against the Vietnam War, and when he was killed in Memphis in April 1968 he was there in support of striking sanitation workers. As Melissa Harris-Lacewell has put it, "Following King meant following the unpopular road, not the popular one."

Moreover, all the features we today identify with freedom and liberal democracy (trade unions, the universal vote, free universal education, freedom of the press, etc.) were won through a long and difficult struggle on the part of the lower classes throughout the nineteenth and twentieth centuries—in other words, they were anything but the "natural" consequences of capitalist relations. Recall the list of demands with which *The Communist Manifesto* concludes: most of them, with the exception of the abolition of private ownership of the means of production, are today widely accepted in "bourgeois" democracies, but only as the result of popular struggles. It is worth underlining another often ignored fact: today, equality between whites and blacks is celebrated as part of the American Dream, and treated as a self-evident politico-ethical axiom; but in the 1920s and 1930s, the US

---

23   This quote and the following two (by Sitkoff and Harris-Lacewell) are taken from an Associated Press report entitled "MLK's legacy is more than his 'Dream' speech," available online at http://*wcbstv.com*.

Communists were the *only* political force to argue for complete racial equality.[24] Those who claim a natural link between capitalism and democracy are cheating with the facts in the same way the Catholic Church cheats when it presents itself as the "natural" advocate of democracy and human rights against the threat of totalitarianism—as if it were not the case that the Church accepted democracy only at the end of the nineteenth century, and even then with clenched teeth, as a desperate compromise, making it clear that it preferred monarchy, and that it was making a reluctant concession to new times.

On account of its all-pervasiveness, ideology appears as its own opposite, as *non-ideology*, as the core of our human identity underneath all the ideological labels. This is why Jonathan Littell's outstanding *Les bienveillantes (The Kindly Ones)*[25] is so traumatic, especially for Germans: it provides a fictional first-person account of the Holocaust from the perspective of a German participant, SS *Obersturmbannführer* Maximilian Aue. The problem is the following: how to render the manner in which the Nazi executioners experienced and symbolized their predicament without engendering sympathy or even justifying them? What Littell offers, to put it in somewhat tasteless terms, is a fictionalized Nazi version of Primo Levi. As such, he has a key Freudian lesson to teach us: one should reject the idea that the proper way to fight the demonization of the Other is to subjectivize him, to listen to his story, to understand how he perceives the situation (or, as a partisan of Middle East dialogue puts it: "An enemy is someone whose story you have not yet heard"). There is, however, a clear limit to this procedure: can one imagine inviting a brutal Nazi thug—like Littell's Maximilian Aue, who rather invites himself—to tell us his story? Is one then also ready to affirm that Hitler was an enemy only because his story had not been heard? Do the details of his personal life "redeem" the horrors that resulted from his reign, do they make him "more human"? To cite one of my favorite examples, Reinhard Heydrich, the architect of the

---

24   See Glenda Elizabeth Gilmore, *Defying Dixie: The Radical Roots of Civil Rights*, New York: Norton 2007.

25   See Jonathan Littell, *The Kindly Ones*, New York: Harper Book Club 2009.

Holocaust, liked to play Beethoven's late string quartets with friends during his evenings of leisure. Our most elementary experience of subjectivity is that of the "richness of my inner life": this is what I "really am," in contrast to the symbolic determinations and responsibilities I assume in public life (as father, professor, etc.). The first lesson of psychoanalysis here is that this "richness of inner life" is fundamentally fake: it is a screen, a false distance, whose function is, as it were, to save my appearance, to render palpable (accessible to my imaginary narcissism) my true social-symbolic identity. One of the ways to practise the critique of ideology is therefore to invent strategies for unmasking this hypocrisy of the "inner life" and its "sincere" emotions. The experience we have of our lives from within, the story we tell ourselves about ourselves in order to account for what we are doing, is thus a lie—the truth lies rather outside, in what we do. Therein resides the difficult lesson of Littell's book: in it, we meet someone whose story we *do* fully hear but who should nonetheless *remain* our enemy. What is truly unbearable about the Nazi executioners is not so much the terrifying things they did, as how "human, all too human" they remained while doing those things. "Stories we tell ourselves about ourselves" serve to obfuscate the true ethical dimension of our acts. In making ethical judgments, we should be story-blind—this is why Elfriede Jelinek's advice to theatre writers is not only aesthetically correct, but has a deep ethical justification:

> Characters on stage should be flat, like clothes in a fashion show: what you get should be no more than what you see. Psychological realism is repulsive, because it allows us to escape unpalatable reality by taking shelter in the "luxuriousness" of personality, losing ourselves in the depth of individual character. The writer's task is to block this manoeuvre, to chase us off to a point from which we can view the horror with a dispassionate eye.[26]

---

26 Elfriede Jelinek, quoted in Nicholas Spice, "Up from the Cellar," *London Review of Books*, June 5, 2008, p. 6.

The same strategy of ideological "humanization" (in the sense of the proverbial wisdom "it is human to err") is a key constituent of the ideological (self-)presentation of the Israeli Defense Forces (IDF). The Israeli media love to dwell on the imperfections and psychic traumas of the Israeli soldiers, presenting them neither as perfect military machines nor as superhuman heroes, but as ordinary people who, caught up in the traumas of History and warfare, sometimes make errors and lose their way. For example, when in January 2003 the IDF demolished the family home of a suspected "terrorist," they did so with accentuated kindness, even helping the family to move their furniture out before destroying the house with a bulldozer. A similar incident was reported a little bit earlier in the Israeli press: when an Israeli soldier was searching a Palestinian house for suspects, the mother of the family called her daughter by her name in order to calm her down, and the surprised soldier learned that the frightened girl's name was the same as that of his own daughter; in a sentimental outburst, he pulled out his wallet and showed her picture to the Palestinian mother. It is easy to discern the falsity of such a gesture of empathy: the notion that, in spite of political differences, we are all basically human beings with the same loves and worries neutralizes the impact of the activity the soldier was engaged in. As such, the only proper reply of the mother should have been: "If you really are a human being like me, *why are you doing what you are doing now*?" The soldier could then only have taken refuge in reified duty: "I don't like it, but it is my duty . . ."—thus avoiding the subjective assumption of his duty.

The point of such humanization is to emphasize the gap between the complex reality of the person and the role he has to play against his true nature. "In my family, our genes are not military," as one of the soldiers interviewed in Claude Lanzmann's *Tsahal* (1994) says, surprised to find himself a career officer.[27] Ironically, Lanzmann here follows the same technique of humanization as does Spielberg, the object of Lanzmann's utter contempt. As in *Shoah*, in *Tsahal* Lanzmann works entirely in the

---

27   "Tsahal" is a Hebrew acronym for the Israeli Defense Forces.

present tense, refusing any archival battle scenes or narration that would provide some historical context. From the very beginning of the film we are thrown *in medias res*: various officers recall the horrors of the 1973 war, while, in the background, we see audio-machines reproducing authentic recordings of what went on at the moment of panic, when Israeli units on the eastern side of the Suez canal were overrun by Egyptian soldiers. This "soundscape" is used as a trigger to transport the interviewed (ex-)soldiers back into their traumatic experience: sweating, they relive the situation in which many of their comrades were killed, and react by fully admitting their human frailty, panic and fear—many of them openly admit that they feared not only for their lives, but for the very existence of Israel itself. Another aspect of this humanization is the intimate "animistic" relationship to weapons, especially tanks. As one of the interviewed soldiers puts it: "They have souls. If you give a tank your love, your care, it will give you everything back."

Lanzmann's focus on the Israeli soldiers' experience of a permanent state of emergency and the threat of annihilation is usually cited to justify the exclusion of the Palestinians' perspective from the film: they are seen only late on, reduced to the non-subjectivized background. The film does show how the Palestinians are *de facto* treated as an underclass, subjected to military and police controls and detained by bureaucratic procedures; but the only explicit critique of Israeli politics in the film is that formulated by Israeli writers and lawyers (Avigdor Feldman, David Grossman, Amos Oz). On a benevolent reading, one could claim (as Janet Maslin did in her *New York Times* review of *Tsahal*) that "Lanzmann lets these faces speak for themselves," letting the oppression of the Palestinians appear as a background presence, all the more overwhelming in its silence. But is it really so? Here is Maslin's description of a key scene towards the end of the film, when Lanzmann engages in debate with an Israeli building contractor:

"When the Arabs know there will be Jews here for eternity, they will learn to live with it," insists this man, whose new houses are being erected on occupied territory. Arab workmen labor busily behind him as he speaks. Confronted by the thorny questions that his settlement-building work raises, the man contradicts himself freely. He also digs in his heels. "This is the land of Israel," he insists obliquely, whenever Mr. Lanzmann, who has made it his mission to explore the Israeli people's relationship with this land, poses one of the many questions that have no answers. Eventually, the director finally gives up arguing, smiles philosophically and throws his arms around the builder. At that moment, he expresses all the ruefulness and frustration seen in *Tsahal* and does it in a single gesture.[28]

Would Lanzmann also "smile philosophically and throw his arms around" the Palestinian laborer in the background, were the latter to express a destructive rage against the Israelis for having reduced him to a paid instrument of the expropriation of his own land? Therein resides the ideological ambiguity of *Tsahal*: the interviewed soldiers play the role of their "ordinary human selves," they embody the masks they have constructed to humanize their acts—an ideological mystification that reaches its unsurpassable ironic peak when Ariel Sharon appears as a peaceful farmer.

It is interesting to note how a similar "humanization" process is increasingly present in the recent wave of blockbusters about superheroes (*Spiderman, Batman, Hancock . . .*). Critics rave about how these films move beyond the original flat comic-book characters and dwell in detail over the uncertainties, weaknesses, doubts, fears and anxieties of the supernatural hero, his struggle with his inner demons, his confrontation with his own dark side, and so forth, as if all this makes the commercial super-production somehow more "artistic." (The exception in this series is M. Night Shyamalan's outstanding *Unbreakable*.)

In real life, this humanization process undoubtedly reached its apogee in a recent North Korean press release which reported that, at the opening game on the country's first golf course, the beloved

---

28 Janet Maslin, "*Tsahal*: Lanzmann's meditation on Israel's defense," *New York Times*, January 27, 1995.

president Kim Jong-Il excelled, finishing the entire game of 18 holes in 19 strikes. One can well imagine the reasoning of the propaganda bureaucrat: nobody was going to believe that Kim had managed a hole-in-one every time, so, to make things realistic, let us concede that, just once, he needed two strikes to succeed . . .

Unfortunately, the same kind of "humanization" ruins *The Baader Meinhof Complex* (2008), the otherwise interesting depiction of the fate of the first-generation Red Army Faction group (Ulrike Meinhof, Gudrun Ensslin, Andreas Baader) in Germany. The subjective standpoint of the film, the position implicitly offered to the spectator as the point of identification, is that of Meinhof, a "terrorist" who nonetheless remains "human," beset by fears and doubts, engaged in constant reflection on her predicament, in contrast with Ensslin and Baader who are presented as brutally inhuman in their "angelic" perfection. The gap that separates them appears at its clearest in their respective suicides: Meinhof hangs herself in despair, as her entire ethico-political universe falls apart, while Ensslin and Baader take their own lives as a coldly planned political statement. (In this respect, Meinhof is the counterpoint to the chief police investigator coordinating the hunt for the terrorists, played by Bruno Ganz: in contrast to his colleagues, who just want to exterminate the terrorists, the chief also reflects on the causes of terror and shows consideration for the wider ideologico-political context.)

We should fearlessly extend this insight into the problematic of false "humanization" to the very basic collective form of "telling stories about ourselves," to the symbolic texture which provides the foundation of a community (ethnic, lifestyle, sexual, religious. . .). Kant's distinction between the public and private uses of reason can be of great help here: the key problem with forms of so-called "identity politics" is that they focus on "private" identities—the ultimate horizon is that of the tolerance and intermingling of such identities, and every universality, every feature that cuts across the entire field, is rejected as oppressive. Paulinian universality, in contrast, is a struggling form. When Paul says, "There are no Greeks or Jews, no men or women . . . ," this does not mean that we are all one happy human family, but rather that there is one big divide which cuts across all these particular identities, rendering them ultimately irrelevant: "There are no Greeks or Jews, no men or women . . . *there are only Christians and the enemies of Christianity!*" Or, as we would have to put it today: there are only those who fight for emancipation and their reactionary opponents; the people and the enemies of the people.

No wonder that the topic of "toxic subjects" has been gaining ground recently. In her book *Toxic People*, Lillian Glass identifies 30 types of such people, some with humorous labels such as "the Smiling Two-Faced Sneaky Back-Stabber."[29] She provides a Toxic People Quiz to help readers identify which category a suspect toxic terror falls into and suggests ten techniques for handling them, including Humor, Direct Confrontation, Calm Questioning, Give-Them-Hell-and-Yell, Love and Kindness, Vicarious Fantasy, etc. Conceding that, to some degree, we are all toxic, Glass also offers a "Toxic Image Inventory" enabling us to identify our own destructive forms of behavior.

Albert J. Bernstein goes a (rhetorical) step further, mobilizing horror-mythology and speaking directly of emotional vampires preying on us whilst masquerading as ordinary people—they may lurk in your office, your family, your circle of friends; they may even share your bed.[30] Bright, talented, and charismatic, they win your trust and affection, and then drain you of your emotional energy. Their main categories include self-serving Narcissists, Hedonistic Antisocials, Exhausting Paranoids, and over-the-top Histrionic Drama Queens. As might be expected, Bernstein also offers a range of defense strategies guaranteed to keep such blood-sucking creatures of darkness from sucking you dry.

The topic of "toxic subjects" is expanding much further, beyond its immediate reference to interpersonal relations. In a paradigmatic "post-modern" way, the predicate "toxic" now covers a series of properties which may belong to totally different levels (natural, cultural, psychological, political). Hence, a "toxic subject" might be an immigrant with a deadly

---

29 See Lillian Glass, *Toxic People*, New York: Simon & Schuster 1995.

30 See Albert J. Bernstein, *Emotional Vampires: Dealing With People Who Drain You Dry*, New York: McGraw-Hill 2002.

disease who should be quarantined; a terrorist whose deadly plans need to be foiled and who belongs in Guantanamo; a fundamentalist ideologist who should be silenced because he is spreading hatred; or a parent, teacher or priest who abuses and corrupts children.

But in a Hegelian gesture of universalization, one should accomplish here the passage from predicate to subject: from the standpoint of the autonomous free subject, is there not something "toxic" about the very idea of a parent, this parasitic mediator who subjects the subject to an authority in the very process of establishing it as free and autonomous? If there is a clinical lesson to be learned about parenthood, it is that there can be no clean, non-toxic parent: some libidinal dirt will always stain the ideal parental figure. And one should push this generalization to the end: what is toxic is ultimately the Neighbor as such, the abyss of its desire and its obscene enjoyment. The ultimate aim of all rules governing interpersonal relations, then, is to quarantine or neutralize this toxic dimension, to reduce the Neighbor to a fellow man. It is thus not enough to search for contingent toxic components in (another) subject, for the subject *as such* is toxic in its very form, in its abyss of Otherness—what makes it toxic is the *objet petit a* on which the subject's consistency hinges. When we think we really know a close friend or relative, it often happens that, all of a sudden, this person does something—utters an unexpectedly vulgar or cruel remark, makes an obscene gesture, casts a cold indifferent glance where compassion was expected—which makes us aware that we do not really know them; we become conscious of a total stranger in front of us. At this point, the fellow man changes into a Neighbor.

As if in an ironic nod to Giorgio Agamben's theory of the state of exception, in July 2008 the Italian government proclaimed a state of emergency throughout Italy in order to cope with the problem of the Neighbor in its paradigmatic contemporary form: the illegal entry of immigrants from North Africa and Eastern Europe. Taking a demonstrative step further in this direction, at the beginning of August, it deployed 4,000 armed soldiers to control sensitive points in big cities (train stations, commercial centers . . .) and thus raise the level of public security. There are also now plans to use the military to protect women from rapists. What is important to note here is that the emergency state was introduced without any great fuss: life goes on as normal . . . Is this not the state we are approaching in developed countries around the globe, where this or that form of the emergency state (deployed against the terrorist threat, against immigrants, and so on) is simply accepted as a measure necessary to guarantee the normal run of things?

So what is the reality of this emergency state? An incident on September 20, 2007—when seven Tunisian fishermen went on trial in Sicily for the crime of rescuing forty-four African migrants from certain death in the sea—will make it clear. If convicted for "aiding and abetting illegal immigrants," they faced between one and fifteen years in jail. On August 7, the fishermen had dropped anchor on a shelf 30 miles south of the island of Lampedusa near Sicily, and fallen sleep. Awakened by screams, they saw a rubber boat crammed with starving people, including women and children, wallowing in the rough waves and on the point of sinking. The captain decided to bring them to the nearest port on Lampedusa, where he and his entire crew were then arrested. All observers agree that the true goal of this absurd trial is to dissuade other boat crews from doing the same thing: no action was taken against other fishermen who, when they found themselves in a similar situation, were reported as having beaten the migrants away with sticks, letting them drown.[31] What this incident demonstrates is that Agamben's notion of *homo sacer*, the one excluded from the civil order who can be killed with impunity, is fully operative in the heart of the very Europe that sees itself as the ultimate bastion of human rights and humanitarian aid, in contrast to the US and the excesses of the "war on terror". The only heroes in this affair were the Tunisian fisher-men, whose captain, Abdelkarim Bayoudh, simply stated: "I'm happy about what I did."

---

31   See the report by Peter Popham, "Tunisian fishermen face 15 years' jail in Italy for saving migrants from rough seas," *Independent*, September 20, 2007, p. 30.

The formula of "reasonable anti-Semitism" was best formulated back in 1938 by Robert Brasillach, who saw himself as a "moderate" anti-Semite:

> We grant ourselves permission to applaud Charlie Chaplin, a half Jew, at the movies; to admire Proust, a half Jew; to applaud Yehudi Menuhin, a Jew; and the voice of Hitler is carried over radio waves named after the Jew Hertz. . . . We don't want to kill anyone, we don't want to organize any pogrom. But we also think that the best way to hinder the always unpredictable actions of instinctual anti-Semitism is to organize a reasonable anti-Semitism.[32]

Is not this same attitude at work in the way our governments are dealing with the "immigrant threat"? After righteously rejecting populist racism as "unreasonable" and unacceptable given our democratic standards, they endorse "reasonably" racist protective measures . . . Like latter-day Brasillachs, some of them, even the Social Democrats, tell us: "We grant ourselves permission to applaud African and East European sportsmen, Asian doctors, Indian software programmers. We don't want to kill anyone, we don't want to organize any pogrom. But we also think that the best way to hinder the always unpredictable actions of violent anti-immigration protests is to organize reasonable anti-immigrant protection." This vision of the detoxification of the Neighbor presents a clear passage from direct barbarism to Berlusconian barbarism with a human face.

The figure of Berlusconi as a "human, all too human" leader is crucial here, since Italy today is effectively a kind of experimental laboratory of our future. If our political scene is split between permissive-liberal technocracy and fundamentalist populism, Berlusconi's great achievement is to have united the two, to have captured both at the same time. It is arguably this combination which makes him unbeatable, at least in the near future; the remains of the Italian "Left" now resignedly accept

---

32   Quoted by Radbod, "Challenging Mind," available online at http://www.europa-landofheroes.com.

him as Fate. This silent acceptance of Berlusconi as Fate is perhaps the saddest aspect of his reign: his democracy is a democracy of those who, as it were, win by default, who rule through cynical demoralization.

What makes Berlusconi so interesting as a political phenomenon is the fact that he, as the most powerful politician in his country, acts more and more shamelessly: he not only ignores or neutralizes any legal investigation into the criminal activity that has allegedly supported his private business interests, he also systematically undermines the basic dignity associated with being the head of state. The dignity of classical politics is grounded in its elevation above the play of particular interests in civil society: politics is "alienated" from civil society, it presents itself as the ideal sphere of the *citoyen* in contrast to the conflict of selfish interests that characterize the *bourgeois*. Berlusconi has effectively abolished this alienation: in contemporary Italy, state power is exercised directly by the base *bourgeois* who ruthlessly and openly exploits state power as a way of protecting his economic interests, and who washes the dirty laundry of his private marriage problems in the style of a vulgar *reality show* in front of millions watching on their TV screens.

The last genuinely tragic US president was Richard Nixon. As two outstanding films about him (Oliver Stone's *Nixon* and the recent *Frost/Nixon*) demonstrate, he was a crook, but a crook who fell victim to the gap between his ideals and ambitions and the reality of his acts, and who thus experienced an authentically tragic downfall. With Ronald Reagan (and Carlos Menem in Argentina), a different figure of the president entered the stage, a "Teflon" president whom one is tempted to characterize as post-Oedipal: a "postmodern" president who, being no longer even expected to stick consistently to his electoral program, has thus become impervious to criticism (recall how Reagan's popularity went up after every public appearance, when journalists enumerated his mistakes). This new kind of president mixes (what appear to be) spontaneously naive outbursts with the most ruthless manipulation.

The wager of Berlusconi's indecent vulgarities is, of course, that the people will identify with him insofar as he embodies or enacts the myth-ical image of the average Italian: "I am one of you, a little bit corrupt, in trouble with the law, I fall out with my wife because I am attracted by other women . . ." Even his grandiose enactment of a noble politician, *Il Cavaliere*, is more like a ridiculously operatic poor man's dream of greatness. And yet, this appearance of his being "just an ordinary guy like the rest of us" should not deceive us: beneath the clownish mask there is a mastery of state power functioning with ruthless efficiency. Even if Berlusconi is a clown without dignity, we should therefore not laugh at him too much—perhaps, by doing so, we are already playing his game. His laughter is more like the obscene-crazy laughter of the superhero's enemy from a Batman or Spiderman movie. To get an idea of the nature of his rule, one should imagine something like the Joker from *Batman* in power. The problem is that technocratic administration combined with a clownish façade do not themselves suffice: something more is needed, namely—fear. Here enters Berlusconi's two-headed beast, consisting of the immigrants and the "Communists" (Berlusconi's generic name for anyone who attacks him, inclusive of the British right-of-center liberal journal, *The Economist*).

Oriana Fallaci (who was otherwise rather sympathetic towards Berlus-coni) once wrote: "True power does not need arrogance, a long beard and a barking voice. True power strangles you with silk ribbons, charm, and intelligence." In order to understand Berlusconi, one has only to add to this series a talent for stupid self-mockery. *Kung Fu Panda*, the 2008 cartoon film hit, provides the basic coordinates of the functioning of contemporary ideology. The fat panda bear dreams of becoming a sacred Kung Fu warrior, and when, through blind chance (beneath which, of course, lurks the hand of Destiny), he is chosen to be the hero to save his city, he succeeds . . . However, throughout the film, this pseudo-oriental spiritualism is constantly being under-mined by a vulgar-cynical sense of humor. The surprise is how this continuous self-mockery in no way impedes on the efficiency of the oriental spiritualism—the film ultimately takes the butt of its endless jokes seriously. Similarly with one of my favorite anecdotes regarding Niels Bohr: surprised at seeing a horseshoe above the door of Bohr's country house, the fellow scientist visiting him exclaimed that he did not share the superstitious belief regarding horseshoes keeping evil spirits out of the house, to which Bohr snapped back: "I don't believe in it either. I have it there because I was told that it works even when one doesn't believe in it." This is indeed how ideology functions today: nobody takes democracy or justice seriously, we are all aware of their corrupted nature, but we participate in them, we display our belief in them, because we assume that they work even if we do not believe in them. This is why Berlusconi is our own big Kung Fu Panda. Perhaps the old Marx brothers quip, "This man looks like a corrupt idiot and acts like one, but this should not deceive you—he *is* a corrupt idiot," here stumbles upon its limit: while Berlusconi is what he appears to be, this appearance nonetheless remains deceptive.

The "New Spirit" of Capitalism

The fear of the "toxic" Other is thus the obverse (and the truth) of our empathy with the-other-reduced-to-a-fellow-man—but how did this syndrome arise? Boltanski and Chiapello's *The New Spirit of Capitalism* examines this process in detail, especially apropos France. In a Weberian mode, the book distinguishes three successive "spirits" of capitalism: the first, the entrepreneurial spirit, lasted until the Great Depression of the 1930s; the second took as its ideal not the entrepreneur but the salaried director of the large firm. (It is easy to see here a close parallel with the well-known passage from individualist Protestant-ethic capitalism to the corporate-managerial capitalism of the "organization man."[33]) From the 1970s onwards, a new figure

---

33 For a detailed description of this passage, see Luc Boltanski and Eve Chiapello, *The New Spirit of Capitalism*, London: Verso 2005.

emerged: capitalism began to abandon the hierarchical Fordist structure in the production process and in its place developed a network-based form of organization founded on employee initiative and autonomy in the workplace. Instead of a hierarchical-centralized chain of command, we now see networks with a multitude of participants, with work organized in the form of teams or projects, and with a general mobilization of workers intent on customer satisfaction thanks to their leaders' vision. In such ways, capitalism is transformed and legitimized as an egalitarian project: accentuating auto-poetic interaction and spontaneous self-organization, it has even usurped the far Left's rhetoric of workers' self-management, turning it from an anti-capitalist slogan into a capitalist one.

Insofar as this post-'68 spirit of capitalism forms a specific economic, social and cultural unity, that very unity justifies the name "postmodernism." This is why, although many justified criticisms were made of postmodernism as a new form of ideology, one should nonetheless admit that, when Jean-François Lyotard, in *The Postmodern Condition*, elevated the term from simply naming certain new artistic tendencies (especially in writing and architecture) to designating a new historical epoch, there was an element of authentic *nomination* in his act. "Postmodernism" now effectively functioned as a new Master-Signifier introducing a new order of intelligibility into the confused multiplicity of historical experience.

At the level of consumption, this new spirit is that of so-called "cultural capitalism": we primarily buy commodities neither on account of their utility nor as status symbols; we buy them to get the experience provided by them, we consume them in order to render our lives pleasurable and meaningful. This triad cannot but evoke the Lacanian triad RSI: the Real of direct utility (good healthy food, the quality of a car, etc.), the Symbolic of the status (I buy a certain car to signal my status—the Thorstein Veblen perspective), the Imaginary of pleasurable and meaningful experience. In Paul Verhoeven's dystopia *Total Recall*, an agency offers to install memories of an ideal holiday into the brain—one no longer even has to actually travel to another place, it is much more practical, and cheaper, simply to purchase memories of the trip. Another version of the same principle would be to experience the desired holiday in virtual reality—since what really matters is the experience, why not go only for that, bypassing the clumsy detour through reality? Consumption is supposed to sustain the quality of life, its time should be "quality time"—not the time of alienation, of imitating models imposed by society, of the fear of not being able to "keep up with the Joneses," but the time of the authentic fulfilment of my true Self, of the sensuous play of experience, and of caring for others, through becoming involved in charity or ecology, etc. Here is an exemplary case of "cultural capitalism": the Starbucks ad campaign "It's not just what you're buying. It's what you're buying into." After celebrating the quality of the coffee itself, the ad goes on:

> But, when you buy Starbucks, whether you realize it or not, you're buying into something bigger than a cup of coffee. You're buying into a coffee ethic. Through our Starbucks Shared Planet program, we purchase more Fair Trade coffee than any company in the world, ensuring that the farmers who grow the beans receive a fair price for their hard work. And, we invest in and improve coffee-growing practices and communities around the globe. It's good coffee karma. . . . Oh, and a little bit of the price of a cup of Starbucks coffee helps furnish the place with comfy chairs, good music, and the right atmosphere to dream, work and chat in. We all need places like that these days. . . . When you choose Starbucks, you are buying a cup of coffee from a company that cares. No wonder it tastes so good.[34]

The "cultural" surplus is here spelled out: the price is higher than elsewhere since what you are really buying is the "coffee ethic" which includes care for the environment, social responsibility towards the producers, plus a place where you yourself can participate in communal

---

34 Quoted from the full-page advertisement in *USA Today*, May 4, 2009, p. A9.

life (from the very beginning, Starbucks presented its coffee shops as an ersatz community). And if this is not enough, if your ethical needs are still unsatisfied and you continue to worry about Third World misery, then there are additional products you can buy. Here is the Starbucks description of their "Ethos Water" program:

> Ethos Water is a brand with a social mission—helping children around the world get clean water and raising awareness of the World Water Crisis. Every time you purchase a bottle of Ethos™ water, Ethos Water will contribute US $0.05 (C$0.10 in Canada) toward our goal of raising at least US $10 million by 2010. Through The Starbucks Foundation, Ethos Water supports humanitarian water programs in Africa, Asia and Latin America. To date, Ethos Water grant commitments exceed $6.2 million. These programs will help an estimated 420,000 people gain access to safe water, sanitation and hygiene education.[35]

(No mention here of the fact that a bottle of Ethos Water is 5 cents more expensive in Starbucks than in other similar places . . .) This is how capitalism, at the level of consumption, integrated the legacy of '68, the critique of alienated consumption: *authentic* experience matters. A recent Hilton Hotels publicity campaign consists of a simple claim: "Travel doesn't only get us from place A to place B. It should also make us a better person." Only a decade ago, could one have imagined such an ad appearing? Is this not also the reason we buy organic food? Who really believes that half-rotten and overpriced "organic" apples are really healthier than the non-organic varieties? The point is that, in buying them, we are not merely buying and consuming, we are simultaneously doing something meaningful, showing our capacity for care and our global awareness, participating in a collective project . . . The latest scientific expression of this "new spirit" is the rise of a new discipline: "happiness studies." How is it, however, that in our era of spiritualized hedonism, when the goal of life

---

35   Quoted from http://www.starbucks.com.

is directly defined as happiness, the number of people suffering from anxiety and depression is exploding? It is the enigma of this self-sabotaging of happiness and pleasure which makes Freud's message more pertinent than ever.

As is often the case, a developing Third World country, namely Bhutan, naively spells out the absurd socio-political consequences of this notion of happiness. Already a decade ago, the kingdom of Bhutan decided to focus on measuring Gross National Happiness (GNH) rather than Gross National Product (GNP); the idea was the brainchild of ex-king Jigme Singye Wangchuck, who sought to steer Bhutan into the modern world while preserving its unique identity. With the pressures of globalization and materialism mounting, and the tiny country set for its first ever elections, the immensely popular Oxford-educated new king, 27-year-old Jigme Khesar Namgyel Wangchuck, ordered a state agency to calculate how happy the kingdom's 670,000 people really are. Officials said they had already conducted a survey of around 1,000 people and drawn up a list of parameters for being happy (similar to the development index, tracked by the United Nations). The main concerns were identified as psychological well-being, health, education, good governance, living standards, community vitality, and ecological diversity . . . *this* is cultural imperialism, if there ever was.[36]

In keeping with the new spirit of capitalism, an entire ideologico-historical narrative is constructed in which socialism appears as conservative, hierarchical, and administrative. The lesson of '68 is then "Goodbye Mr. Socialism," and the true revolution that of digital capitalism—itself the logical consequence, indeed the "truth," of the '68 revolt. More radically even, the events of '68 are inscribed into the fashionable topic of the "paradigm shift." The parallel between the model of the brain in neuroscience and the predominant ideological models of society is here indicative.[37] There are clear echoes between

---

36 "Bhutan tries to measure happiness," ABC News, March 24, 2008.

37 See Catherine Malabou, *Que faire de notre cerveau?* Paris: Bayard 2004.

today's cognitivism and "postmodern" capitalism: when Daniel Dennett, for example, advocates a shift from the Cartesian notion of the Self as a central controlling agency of psychic life to a notion of the auto-poetic interaction of competing multiple agents, does this not echo the shift from central bureaucratic control and planning to the network model? It is thus not only that our brain is socialized—society itself is also naturalized in the brain,[38] which is why Malabou is right in emphasizing the need to address the key question: "What is to be done to avoid the consciousness of the brain coinciding directly and simply with the spirit of capitalism?"

Even Hardt and Negri endorse this parallel: in the same way as the brain sciences teach us how there is no central Self, so the new society of the multitude which rules itself will be like today's cognitivist notion of the ego as a pandemonium of interacting agents with no central authority running the show … No wonder Negri's notion of communism comes uncannily close to that of "postmodern" digital capitalism.[39]

Ideologically—and here we come to the crucial point—this shift occurred as a reaction to the revolts of the 1960s (from May '68 in Paris, to the student movement in Germany, and the hippies in the US). The anti-capitalist protests of the '60s supplemented the standard critique of socio-economic exploitation with the new topics of cultural critique: the alienation of everyday life, the commodification of consumption, the inauthenticity of a mass society in which we are forced to "wear masks" and subjected to sexual and other oppressions, etc. The new spirit of capitalism triumphantly recuperated the egalitarian and anti-hierarchical rhetoric of 1968, presenting itself as a successful libertarian revolt against the oppressive social organizations characteristic of both corporate capitalism *and* Really Existing Socialism—a new libertarian spirit epitomized by dressed-down "cool" capitalists such as Bill Gates and the founders of Ben and Jerry's ice cream.

---

38 Ibid., p. 88.
39 See Michael Hardt and Antonio Negri, *Multitude*, London: Penguin Press 2004.

We can now understand why so many insist that Che Guevara, one of the symbols of '68, has become "the quintessential postmodern icon" signifying both everything and nothing—in other words, whatever one wants him to signify: youth rebellion against authoritarianism, solidarity with the poor and exploited, saintliness, up to and including the liberal-communist entrepreneurial spirit of working for the good of all. A couple of years ago, even a high Vatican representative proclaimed that the celebration of Che is to be understood as expressing admiration for a man who risked and gave his life for the good of others. As usually, harmless beatification is mixed with its opposite, obscene commodification—an Australian company recently marketed a "Cherry Guevara" ice cream, focusing its promotion on the "eating experience," of course: "The revolutionary struggle of the cherries was squashed as they were trapped between two layers of chocolate. May their memory live in your mouth!"[40] There is nonetheless something desperate in this insistence that Che has become a neutral commodity logo—witness the series of recent publications warning us that he was also a cold-blooded murderer who orchestrated the purges in Cuba in 1959, and so forth. Significantly, these warnings popped up precisely as new anti-capitalist rebellions began to take place all around the world, making his icon potentially dangerous again. Under the title "Polish Minister Wants Ban on Lenin, Guevara T-Shirts," *Europe News* reported on April 23, 2009 that "Poland's equality minister wants to expand a ban on fascist or totalitarian propaganda to include books, clothing and other items":

Minister Elzbieta Radziszewska wants to widen a law that prohibits producing fascist or totalitarian propaganda. The legislation would prohibit images of Che Guevara, popular across the world on t-shirts, posters and murals. "I support such a solution," Professor Wojciech Roszkowski told the daily *Rzeczpospolita*. "Communism was a terrible,

40 See Michael Glover, "The marketing of a Marxist," *Times* (London), June 6, 2006.

murderous system, responsible for a million victims. It's very similar to National Socialism. There's no reason to treat the systems—and their symbols—any differently."

What survived of the sexual liberation of the 1960s was a tolerant hedonism easily incorporated into our hegemonic ideology standing under the aegis of the superego. So what is the superego? On the information sheet in a New York hotel, I recently read: "Dear guest! To guarantee that you will fully enjoy your stay with us, this hotel is totally smoke-free. For any infringement of this regulation, you will be charged $200." The beauty of this formulation, taken literally, is that you are to be punished for refusing to fully enjoy your stay . . . The superego imperative to enjoy thus functions as the reversal of Kant's "*Du kannst, denn du sollst!*" (You can, because you must!); it relies on a "You must, because you can!" That is to say, the superego aspect of today's "non-repressive" hedonism (the constant provocation we are exposed to, enjoining us to go right to the end and explore all modes of *jouissance*) resides in the way permitted *jouissance* necessarily turns into obligatory *jouissance*. This drive to pure autistic *jouissance* (through drugs or other trance-inducing means) arose at a precise political moment: when the emancipatory sequence of 1968 had exhausted its potential. At this critical point (the mid-1970s), the only option left was a direct, brutal, *passage à l'acte*, a push-towards-the-Real, which assumed three main forms: the search for extreme forms of sexual *jouissance*; Leftist political terrorism (the RAF in Germany, the Red Brigades in Italy, etc., whose wager was that, in an epoch in which the masses have become totally immersed in the capitalist ideological morass, the standard critique of ideology is no longer operative, and only a resort to the raw Real of direct violence— *l'action directe*—will awaken the masses); and, finally, the turn towards the Real of an inner experience (oriental mysticism). What all three shared was the withdrawal from concrete socio-political engagement into a direct contact with the Real.

This shift from political engagement to the post-political Real is perhaps best exemplified by the films of Bernardo Bertolucci, that arch-renegade, whose works range from early masterpieces like *Prima della rivoluzione* to late aestheticist-spiritualist self-indulgences such as the abominable *Little Buddha*. This span achieved full circle with *The Dreamers*, Bertolucci's late film about Paris '68, in which a couple of French students (a brother and sister) befriend a young American student during the whirlwind of the events. By the film's end, however, the friends have split up, after the French students become caught up in the political violence, while the American remains faithful to the message of love and emotional liberation.

Jean-Claude Milner is keenly aware of how the establishment succeeded in undoing all threatening consequences of 1968 by way of incorporating the so-called "spirit of '68" and thereby turning it against the real core of the revolt. The demands for new rights (which would have meant a true redistribution of power) were granted, but merely in the guise of "permissions"—the "permissive society" being precisely one which broadens the scope of what subjects are allowed to do without actually giving them any additional power:

> Those who hold power know very well the difference between a right and a permission. . . . A right in a strict sense of the term gives access to the exercise of a power, at the expense of another power. A permission doesn't diminish the power of the one who gives it; it doesn't augment the power of the one who gets it. It makes his life easier, which is not nothing.[41]

This is how it goes with the right to divorce, abortion, gay marriage, and so on and so forth— these are all permissions masked as rights; they do not change in any way the distribution of powers. Such was the effect of the "spirit of '68": it "effectively contributed to making life easier. This is

---

41 Jean-Claude Milner, *L'arrogance du present. Regards sur une decennie:* 1965–1975, Paris: Grasset 2009, p. 233.

a lot, but it is not everything. Because it didn't encroach upon powers."[42] Therein resides "the secret of the tranquility which has ruled in France over the last forty years":

> the spirit of 68 made itself the best ally of the restoration. Here is the secret of the violence increasingly produced on the margins of the cities: the spirit of 68 now persists only with those who are installed in the cities. The impoverished youth doesn't know what to do with it.[43]

While May '68 aimed at total (and totally politicized) activity, the "spirit of '68" transposed this into a depoliticized pseudo-activity (new life-styles, etc.), the very form of social passivity. One consequence has been the recent outbursts of violence in the suburbs, deprived of any utopian or libertarian content. Milner's bitter conclusion is this: "Do not talk to me anymore about permissions, control, equality; I only know force. Here is my question: in the face of the reconciliation of the notables and the solidarity of the strongest, how to make it that the weak will have powers?"[44]

If the Left withdrew into the intimacies of the sexual or spiritual Real, what happened with the *form* of radical political organization, the semi-illegal groups preparing for the apocalyptic final battle in the interstices of state power? In a way, these cells have resurfaced in the shape of survivalist groups in the US; although their ideological message is one of religious racism, their entire mode of organization (as small illegal groups fighting the FBI and other federal agencies) makes them appear as the uncanny double of the Black Panthers from the 1960s. These weird Hardt-and-Negri-sounding words are from a song accompanying a survivalist-fundamentalist recruitment video from 1982:

---

42   Ibid., p. 236.
43   Ibid., p. 237.
44   Ibid., p. 241.

> Multitudes, multitudes in the valley of decision
> For the day of the LORD is near in the valley of decision.

The irony of the situation is that, with regard to the apocalyptic organizational form of the state of emergency (the collective awareness that they are "living in the last of days"), the survivalist fundamentalists are right. But they are mistaken in their *populist* logic. Populism is ultimately always sustained by the frustrated exasperation of ordinary people, by the cry "I don't know what's going on, but I've just had enough of it! It cannot go on! It must stop!" Such impatient outbursts betray a refusal to understand or engage with the complexity of the situation, and give rise to the conviction that there must be somebody responsible for the mess—which is why some agent lurking behind the scenes is invariably required. Therein, in this refusal-to-know, resides the properly *fetishistic* dimension of populism. That is to say, although at a purely formal level fetishism involves a gesture of transference (onto the object-fetish), it functions as an exact inversion of the standard formula of transference (with the "subject supposed to know"): what fetishism gives body to is precisely my disavowal of knowledge, my refusal to subjectively assume what I know. This is why, to put it in Nietzschean terms which are here highly appropriate, the ultimate difference between a truly radical emancipatory politics and a populist politics is that the former is active, it imposes and enforces its vision, while populism is fundamentally *re*-active, the result of a reaction to a disturbing intruder. In other words, populism remains a version of the politics of fear: it mobilizes the crowd by stoking up fear of the corrupt external agent.

This brings us to the important topic of the blurred relationship between power and knowledge in modern societies. In what Lacan calls the University discourse, authority is exerted by (expert) knowledge. Jacques-Alain Miller is right to point out how Lacan's originality in dealing with the couple knowledge/power was little noticed at the time. In contrast to Foucault, who endlessly varied the motif of their conjunction (knowledge is not neutral, it is in itself an apparatus of power and control), Lacan "poses, for the modern age, disjunction, tearing, discord between knowledge and power. . . . The diagnostic that Lacan poses for the malaise of civilization is that knowledge has assumed 'a disproportionate growth in relationship to the effects of power.'"[45] In the fall of 2007, a public debate raged in the Czech Republic concerning the installation of US Army radars on Czech territory; although a large majority of the population (around 70 percent) was opposed to it, the government pushed on with the project. Government representatives rejected calls for a referendum, arguing that one does not make decisions about such sensitive national security matters merely by voting—they should be left to the military experts.[46] If one follows this logic through to the end, one arrives at a strange result: what *is* there, then, left to vote about? Should not economic decisions, for example, be left to economic experts, and so on for all other realms?

This situation presents us with the deadlock of the contemporary "society of choice" in its most radical form. There are multiple ideological investments in the topic of choice today, even though brain scientists point out that freedom of choice is an illusion—we experience ourselves as "free" simply when we are able to act in the way our organism has determined, with no external obstacles to thwart our inner propensities.[47] Liberal economists emphasize freedom of choice as the key ingredient of the market economy: by buying things we are, in a certain way, continuously voting with our money. "Deeper" existential thinkers

---

45   Ibid.

46   Interestingly, the same representatives evoked a purely political reason for the decision: the US had helped the Czechs to achieve freedom three times in their history (in 1918, 1945, and 1989), so the Czechs should now return the favor by denying themselves this very freedom. . .

47   Recent research has already moved much further than Benjamin Libet's classic experiments from the 1980s, which demonstrated that our brain makes a decision around three tenths of a second before the brain's owner becomes aware of it. By measuring brain activity during a complex problem-solving exercise, one can establish that the volunteer will have the magical momentary insight that solves the problem a full ten seconds before the insight actually occurs to him. See "Incognito," *Economist*, April 18–24, 2009, pp. 78–9.

like to deploy variations on the theme of the "authentic" existential choice, where the very core of our being is at stake—a choice which involves a full existential engagement, as opposed to the superficial choices of this or that commodity. In the "Marxist" version of this theme, the multiplicity of choices with which the market bombards us only serves to obfuscate the absence of any really radical choice concerning the fundamental structure of our society. There is, however, a feature conspicuously missing from this series: namely, the injunction to choose when we lack the basic cognitive coordinates needed to make a rational choice. As Leonardo Padura puts it: "It is horrific not to know the past and yet be able to impact on the future";[48] being compelled to make decisions in a situation which remains opaque is our basic condition. We know the standard situation of the forced choice in which I am free to choose on condition that I make the right choice, so that the only thing left for me to do is make the empty gesture of pretending to accomplish freely what expert knowledge has imposed upon me. But what if, on the contrary, the choice really *is* free and, for this very reason, is experienced as even more frustrating? We thus find ourselves constantly in the position of having to decide about matters that will fundamentally affect our lives, but without a proper foundation in knowledge. To quote John Gray again: "we have been thrown into a time in which everything is provisional. New technologies alter our lives daily. The traditions of the past cannot be retrieved. At the same time we have little idea of what the future will bring. *We are forced to live as if we were free.*"[49]

The incessant pressure to choose involves not only ignorance about the object of choice, but, even more radically, the subjective impossibility of answering the question of desire. When Lacan defines the object of desire as originally lost, his point is not simply that we never know what we desire and are condemned to an eternal search for the

---

48 Leonardo Padura, *Havana Gold*, London: Bitter Lemon Press 2008, pp. 233–4.
49 Gray, *Straw Dogs*, p. 110.

"true" object, which is the void of desire as such, while all positive objects are merely its metonymic stand-ins. His point is a much more radical one: the lost object is ultimately the subject itself, the subject as an object; which means that the question of desire, its original enigma, is not primarily "What do I want?" but "What do others want from me? What object—*objet a*—do they see in me?" Which is why, apropos the hysterical question "Why am I that name?" (i.e., where does my symbolic identity originate, what justifies it?), Lacan points out that the subject as such is hysterical. He defines the subject tautologically as "that which is not an object," the point being that the impossibility of identifying oneself as an object (that is, of knowing what I am libidinally for others) is constitutive of the subject. In this way, Lacan generates the entire diversity of "pathological" subjective positions, reading it as the diversity of the answers to the hysterical question: the hysteric and the obsessive enact two modalities of the question—the psychotic knows itself as the object of the Other's *jouissance*, while the pervert posits itself as the instrument of the Other's *jouissance*.

Herein resides the terrorizing dimension of the pressure to choose—what resonates even in the most innocent inquiry when one reserves a hotel room ("Soft or hard pillows? Double or twin beds?") is the much more radical probing: "Tell me who you are? What kind of an object do you want to be? What would fill in the gap of your desire?" This is why the "anti-essentialist" Foucauldian apprehension about "fixed identities"—the incessant urge to practise the "care of the Self," to continuously re-invent and re-create oneself—finds a strange echo in the dynamics of "postmodern" capitalism. Of course, good old existentialism had already claimed that man is what he makes of himself, and had linked this radical freedom to existential anxiety. Here the anxiety of experiencing one's freedom, the lack of one's substantial determination, was the authentic moment at which the subject's integration into the fixity of its ideological universe is shattered. But what existentialism was not able to envisage is what Adorno endeavored to encapsulate with the title of his book on Heidegger, *Jargon of Authenticity*; namely how, by no longer simply repressing the lack of a fixed identity, the hegemonic ideology directly mobilizes that lack to sustain the endless process of consumerist "self-re-creation."

Between the Two Fetishisms

How is this appearance of ideology as its own opposite, as non-ideology, possible? It hinges on a shift in the predominant mode of ideology: in our allegedly "post-ideological" era, ideology functions more and more in a *fetishistic* mode as opposed to its traditional *symptomal* mode. In the latter mode, the ideological lie which structures our perception of reality is threatened by symptoms *qua* "returns of the repressed"—cracks in the fabric of the ideological lie—while the fetish is effectively a kind of *envers* of the symptom. That is to say, the symptom is the exception which disturbs the surface of the false appearance, the point at which the repressed Other Scene erupts, while the fetish is the embodiment of the Lie which enables us to sustain the unbearable truth. Take the case of the death of a beloved person: in the case of a symptom, I "repress" this death, I try not to think about it, but the repressed trauma returns in the symptom; in the case of a fetish, on the contrary, I "rationally" fully accept the death, and yet I cling to the fetish, to some feature that embodies for me the disavowal of the death. In this sense, a fetish can play the very constructive role of allowing us to cope with a harsh reality: fetishists are not dreamers lost in their own private worlds, they are thoroughgoing "realists," able to accept the way things are because by clinging to their fetish they are able to mitigate the full impact of reality.

In this precise sense, money is, for Marx, a fetish: I pretend to be a rational, utilitarian subject, well aware how things truly stand, but I embody my disavowed belief in the money-fetish ... Sometimes, the line between the two is almost indiscernible: an object can function as a symptom (of a repressed desire) and almost simultaneously as a fetish (embodying the belief we officially renounce). A leftover of the dead person for example, such as an item of their clothing, can function both as a fetish (in it, the person magically continues to live) and as a symptom (the disturbing detail that brings to mind his or her death). Is this ambiguous tension not homologous to that between the phobic and the fetishist object? The structural role is in both cases the same: if this exceptional element is disturbed, the whole system collapses. Not only does the subject's false universe collapse if she is forced to confront the meaning of her symptom; the opposite also holds, i.e. the subject's "rational" acceptance of the way things are dissolves when his fetish is taken away from him.

"Western Buddhism" is just such a fetish: it enables you to fully participate in the frantic capitalist game while sustaining the perception that you are not really in it, that you are well aware how worthless the whole spectacle is, since what really matters is the peace of the inner Self to which you know you can always withdraw . . . In a further specification, one should note that a fetish can function in two opposed ways: on the one hand its role may remain unconscious; on the other, one may think that the fetish is what really matters, as in the case of the Western Buddhist unaware that the "truth" of his existence lies in the very social relations he tends to dismiss as a mere game.

Another distinction between two different modes of fetishism is even more important: the aforementioned permissive-cynical fetishism should be opposed to populist-fascistic fetishism. Let us explain this former mode by, once again, opposing the ideological mystification it involves to populist-fascistic mystification. The first involves a false universality: the subject advocates freedom or equality, while being unaware of implicit qualifications which, in their very form, constrain its scope (the privileging of certain social strata: being rich, or male, or belonging to a certain culture, etc.). The second involves a false identification of both the nature of the antagonism and the enemy: class struggle is displaced, for instance, onto the struggle against the Jews, so that popular rage at being exploited is redirected away from capitalist relations as such and onto the "Jewish plot." So, to put it in naively hermeneutic terms, in the first case, "when the subject says 'freedom and equality,' he *really means* 'freedom of trade, equality before the law,' etc."; and in the second case, "when the subject says 'Jews are the cause of our misery,' he *really means* 'big capital is the cause of our misery.'" The asymmetry is clear. To put it again in naive terms: in the first case, the explicit "good" content (freedom/equality) covers up the implicit "bad" content (class and other privileges and exclusions), while in the second case, the explicit "bad" content (anti-Semitism) covers over the implicit "good" content (class struggle, hatred of exploitation).

As we can clearly see, the inner structure of these two ideological mystifications is again that of the couple *symptom/fetish*: the implicit limitations (on freedom/equality) are the symptoms of liberal egalitarianism (singular returns of the repressed truth), whilst the "Jew" is the fetish of anti-Semitic fascists (the "last thing the subject sees" before confronting class struggle). This asymmetry has crucial consequences for the critico-ideological process of demystification: apropos liberal egalitarianism, it is not enough to make the old Marxist point about the gap between the ideological appearance of the universal legal form and the particular interests that effectively sustain it, as is so common among politically correct critics on the Left. The counter-argument that the form is never a "mere form," but has a dynamic of its own which leaves traces in the materiality of social life, as developed by theoreticians such as Claude Lefort[50] and Jacques Rancière,[51] is fully valid—it was bourgeois "formal freedom" which set in motion the process of "material" political demands and practises, from trade unionism to feminism. One should resist the cynical temptation of reducing it to a mere illusion concealing a different actuality; this would be to fall into the trap of the old Stalinist hypocrisy which mocked "merely formal" bourgeois freedom—if it was so merely formal as to be incapable of disturbing the true power relations, why then did the Stalinist regime not allow such freedom? Why was it so afraid of it?

---

50 See Claude Lefort, *The Political Forms of Modern Society: Bureaucracy, Democracy, Totalitarianism*, Cambridge: MIT Press 1986.

51 See Jacques Rancière, *Hatred of Democracy*, London: Verso Books 2007.

The interpretive demystification is here thus relatively easy, since it mobilizes the tension between form and content: to be consistent, an "honest" liberal democrat will have to admit that the content of his ideological premise belies its form, and thus will radicalize the form (the egalitarian axiom) by way of implementing the content more thoroughly. (The main alternative is the retreat into cynicism: "we know egalitarianism is an impossible dream, so let us pretend that we are egalitarians, while silently accepting the necessary limitations . . .")

In the case of the "Jew" as the fascistic fetish, the interpretive demystification is much more difficult (thereby confirming the clinical insight that a fetishist cannot be undermined with an interpretation of the "meaning" of his fetish—fetishists feel satisfied in their fetishes, they experience no need to be rid of them). In practical political terms, this means that it is almost impossible to "enlighten" an exploited worker who blames "the Jews" for his misery—explaining to him how the "Jew" is the wrong enemy, promoted by his true enemy (the ruling class) in order to obscure the true struggle—and thus to direct his attention away from "Jews" and towards "capitalists." (Even empirically, while many communists joined the Nazis in Germany in the 1920s and 1930s, and while many disappointed communist voters in France over the last few decades have turned to Le Pen's National Front, the opposite process has been extremely rare.) To put it in crude political terms, the paradox is thus that, while the subject of the first mystification is primarily the enemy (the liberal "bourgeois" who thinks he is fighting for universal equality and freedom), and while the subjects of the second mystification are primarily "our own" (the underprivileged themselves, who are seduced into directing their rage at the wrong target), effective and practical "demystification" is much easier in the first case than in the second.

The contemporary hegemonic ideological scene is thus split between these two modes of fetishism, the cynical and the fundamentalist, both impervious to "rational" argumentative criticism. While the fundamentalist ignores (or at least mistrusts) argumentation, blindly clinging to his fetish, the cynic pretends to accept argumentation, but ignores its symbolic efficiency. In other words, while the fundamentalist (not so much believes as) directly "knows" the truth embodied in his fetish, the cynic practises the logic of disavowal ("I know very well, but . . ."). We can thus construct a matrix consisting of four positions (or attitudes towards ideology): (1) liberal, (2) cynical fetishist, (3) fundamentalist fetishist; (4) ideologico-critical. Unsurprisingly, they form a Greimasian semiotic square in which the four positions are distributed along two axes: symptom versus fetish; identification versus distance. Both the liberal and the critic-of-ideology move at the symptomal level: the first is caught up in it, the second undermines it by way of interpretive analysis. Both the populist fetishist and the cynic cling to their fetish: the first directly, the second in a disavowed manner. Both the populist fetishist and the liberal directly identify with their position (clinging to their fetish; taking seriously the arguments for their universal ideological claims), while both the cynic and the critic-of-ideology distance themselves from their position (fetishistic disavowal or critical interpretation).

With regard to ideological struggle then, this means that one should at least view with profound suspicion those Leftists who argue that the Muslim fundamentalist-populist movements, as emancipatory and anti-imperialist, are basically "on our side," and that the fact that they formulate their programs in directly anti-Enlightenment and anti-universalistic terms, sometimes approaching explicit anti-Semitism, is no more than a confusion resulting from their being caught up into the immediacy of struggle. ("When they say they are against the Jews, what they really mean is only that they are against Zionist colonialism.") One should unconditionally resist the temptation to "understand" Arab anti-Semitism (where we really encounter it) as a "natural" reaction to the sad plight of the Palestinians: there should be no "understanding" of the fact that in several Arab countries Hitler is still considered a hero by many, or of the fact that in their primary school textbooks all the traditional anti-Semitic myths are recycled, from the notorious forgery The Protocols of the Elders of Zion to the idea that Jews use the blood of Christian (or Arab) children for sacrificial purposes. To claim that such anti-Semitism articulates in a displaced mode a form of resistance to capitalism in no way justifies it: displacement is here not a secondary operation, but the fundamental gesture of ideological mystification. What this claim *does* involve, however, is the idea that in the long term the only way to fight anti-Semitism is not to preach liberal tolerance and the like, but to articulate its underlying anti-capitalist motivation in a direct and non-displaced way. To accept the aforementioned erroneous logic of fundamentalism is to take the first step on a path towards the quite "logical" conclusion that, since Hitler also "really meant" capitalists when he spoke of "Jews," he should be our strategic ally in the global anti-imperialist struggle, with the Anglo-American empire as the principal enemy. (And this line of reasoning is not a mere rhetorical exercise: the Nazis did promote anti-colonialist struggle in Arab countries and in India, and many neo-Nazis do sympathize with the Arab struggle against the State of Israel.)[52] It would be a fatal mistake to think that, at some point in the future, we will convince the fascists that their "real" enemy is capital, and that they should drop the particular religious/ethnic/racist form of their ideology in order to join forces with egalitarian universalism.

Thus one should clearly reject the dangerous motto "the enemy of my enemy is my friend," which leads us to discern "progressive" anti-imperialist potential in fundamentalist Islamist movements. The ideological universe of organizations like Hezbollah is based on the blurring of distinctions between capitalist neo-imperialism and secular progressive emancipation: within the ideological space of Hezbollah, women's emancipation, gay rights, and so on, are *nothing but* "decadent" moral aspects of Western imperialism ... Badiou concedes that "there is an internal limitation to these movements, bound as they are to religious particularity"—but is this limitation only a temporary one, as Badiou seems to imply, a limit these movements will (have to)

---

52   What makes the unique figure of Jacques Vergès, the "advocate of terror," a universal phenomenon is that he embodies this "solidarity" between fascism and anti-colonialism.

overcome in the proverbial "second, higher" stage of their development, when they will (have to) universalize themselves? Badiou is right
to note that the problem here is not religion as such, but its particularity—but is this particularity not *right now* a fatal limitation of these
movements, whose ideology is directly anti-Enlightenment?

More precisely, one should specify that the internal limitation
concerns not their religious character as such, no matter how "fundamentalist" it is, but their practico-ideological attitude towards the
universalist emancipatory project based upon the axiom of equality.
To make this key point clear, let us recall the tragic case of the Canudos
community in Brazil at the end of the nineteenth century: this was a
"fundamentalist" community if there ever was one, run by a fanatic
"Councillor" advocating theocracy and a return to monarchy. But at
the same time it sought to create a communist utopia with communal
property, no money or laws, full egalitarian solidarity, equality between
men and women, the right to divorce, etc. It is this dimension that is
lacking in Muslim "fundamentalism," no matter how "anti-imperialist"
it pretends to be.

Nonetheless, even in the case of "clearly" fundamentalist movements,
one should be careful not to trust the bourgeois media. The Taliban are
regularly presented as a fundamentalist Islamist group who enforce their
rule with the use of terror. However, when in the spring of 2009 they took
over the Swat valley in Pakistan, the *New York Times* reported that they
had engineered "a class revolt that exploits profound fissures between a
small group of wealthy landlords and their landless tenants":

> In Swat, accounts from those who have fled now make clear that the
> Taliban seized control by pushing out about four dozen landlords who
> held the most power. To do so, the militants organized peasants into
> armed gangs that became their shock troops. . . . The Taliban's ability to
> exploit class divisions adds a new dimension to the insurgency and is
> raising alarm about the risks to Pakistan, which remains largely feudal.

Mahboob Mahmood, a Pakistani-American lawyer and former

classmate of President Obama's, said, "The people of Pakistan are psychologically ready for a revolution." Sunni militancy is taking advantage of deep class divisions that have long festered in Pakistan. "The militants, for their part, are promising more than just proscriptions on music and schooling," he said. "They are also promising Islamic justice, effective government and economic redistribution."[53]

Thomas Altizer[54] spelled out the implications and consequences of this new (to our Western ears) data:

Now it is finally being revealed that the Taliban is a genuine liberating force assaulting an ancient feudal rule in Pakistan and freeing the vast peasant majority from that rule. . . . Hopefully we will now hear genuine criticism of the Obama administration which is far more dangerous than the Bush administration both because it is being given such a free hand and because it is a far stronger administration.

The ideological bias in the *New York Times* article is discernible in how it speaks of the Taliban's "ability to exploit class divisions," as if the Taliban's "true" agenda lies elsewhere—in religious fundamentalism—and they are merely "taking advantage" of the plight of the poor landless farmers. To this, one should simply add two things. First, this distinction between the "true" agenda and the instrumental manipulation is an externally imposed one: as if the poor landless farmers themselves do not experience their plight in "fundamentalist religious" terms! Second, if by "taking advantage" of the farmers' plight the Taliban are "raising alarm about the risks to Pakistan, which remains largely feudal," what prevents liberal democrats in Pakistan as well as in the US from similarly "taking advantage" of the situation and trying to help the landless farmers? The sad truth behind the fact that this obvious question is not raised in the

---

53   Jane Perlez and Pir Zubair Shah, "Taliban exploit class rifts to gain ground in Pakistan," *New York Times*, April 16, 2009.

54   Thomas Altizer, quoted from personal communication.

New York Times report is that the feudal forces in Pakistan are themselves the "natural ally" of liberal democracy . . .

One of the political consequences of this paradoxical situation is the properly dialectical tension between long-term strategy and short-term tactical alliances. Although, in the long term, the success of the radical emancipatory struggle depends on mobilizing the lower classes who are today often in thrall to fundamentalist populism, one should have no qualms about concluding short-term alliances with egalitarian liberals as part of the anti-sexist and anti-racist struggle.

What phenomena such as the rise of the Taliban demonstrate is that Walter Benjamin's old thesis that "every rise of Fascism bears witness to a failed revolution" not only still holds true today, but is perhaps more pertinent than ever. Liberals like to point out similarities between Left and Right "extremisms": Hitler's terror and death camps imitated Bolshevik terror and the Gulags; the Leninist form of the party is kept alive today in al-Qaeda—yes, but what does all this mean? It can also be read as an indication of how fascism literally replaces (takes the place of) Leftist revolution: its rise is the Left's failure, but simultaneously a proof that there was a revolutionary potential, a dissatisfaction, which the Left was not able to mobilize. And does the same not hold for so-called "Islamo-Fascism"? Is the rise of radical Islamism not exactly correlative to the disappearance of the secular Left in Muslim countries? Today, when Afghanistan is portrayed as the epitome of a fundamentalist Islamist country, who still remembers that, only 30 years ago, it was a country with strong secular tradition, including a powerful Communist Party which took power independently of the Soviet Union? Where did this secular tradition go? In Europe, exactly the same goes for Bosnia: back in the 1970s and 1980s, Bosnia and Herzegovina was (multi)culturally the most interesting and lively of all Yugoslav republics, with an internationally recognized cinema school and a unique style of rock music. Today's Bosnia, by contrast, is marked by powerful fundamentalist forces, such as the Muslim crowd which brutally attacked the gay parade in Sarajevo in September 2008. The root cause of this regression lies in the desperate situation of Bosnian Muslims during the 1992–95 war, when they were basically abandoned by the Western powers to the Serb guns.

Furthermore, are the terms "Islamo-Fascism" or "Fascismo-Islamism," proposed by (amongst others) Francis Fukuyama and Bernard-Henri Lévy, justified? What renders them problematic is not only the religious qualification (is one then also ready to describe Western forms of fascism as "Christo-Fascism"?—fascism in itself is enough, it needs no qualifiers), but the very designation of contemporary "fundamentalist" Islamic movements and states as "fascist." It may be a fact that (more or less open) anti-Semitism is present in these movements and states, and that there are historical links between Arab nationalism and European fascism and Nazism. However, anti-Semitism does not play in Muslim fundamentalism the exact role it plays in European fascism—where the emphasis is on the external intruder responsible for the disintegration of one's own (once) "harmonious" society. There is at least one big difference which cannot but strike the eye. For the Nazis, the Jews were a nomadic/stateless/rootless people corrupting the communities within which they lived; as such, from a Nazi perspective, a State of Israel was a possible solution—no wonder that, before deciding to exterminate them, the Nazis played with the idea of giving the Jews a land to form a state (with the loci ranging from Madagascar to Palestine itself). For today's "anti-Zionist" Arabs, on the contrary, it is the *State* of Israel which is the problem, with some calling for the destruction of that state and a return of the Jews to their stateless/nomadic condition.

We all know the anti-communist characterization of Marxism as "the Islam of twentieth century," a secularization of Islam's abstract fanaticism. Pierre-André Taguieff, the liberal historian of anti-Semitism, has turned this characterization around: Islam is turning out to be "the Marxism of twenty-first century," prolonging, after the decline of communism, its violent anti-capitalism. If we take into account Benjamin's idea of fascism occupying the place of the failed revolution, the "rational core" of such inversions can easily be accepted by Marxists. However, it would be totally wrong to draw from this the conclusion that the most the Left can do is hope that the crisis will be limited, and that capitalism will continue to guarantee a relatively high standard of living for a growing number of people—a strange radical politics whose main hope is that circumstances will continue to render it inoperative and marginal . . . This seems to be the conclusion drawn by some Leftists such as Moishe Postone and his colleagues: since every crisis which opens up a space for the radical Left also gives rise to anti-Semitism, it is better for us to support successful capitalism and hope there will be no crisis. Taken to its logical conclusion, this reasoning implies that, ultimately, anti-capitalism is, as such, anti-Semitic. It is against such reasoning that one has to read Badiou's motto "*mieux vaut un désastre qu'un désêtre*": one has to take the risk of fidelity to an Event, even if the Event ends up in an "obscure disaster." The best indicator of the Left's lack of trust in itself is its fear of crisis; such a Left fears for its own comfortable position as a critical voice fully integrated into the system, ready to risk nothing. Which is why today, more than ever, Mao Zedong's old motto is pertinent: "Everything under heaven is in utter chaos; the situation is excellent."

A true Left takes a crisis seriously, without illusions, but as something inevitable, as a chance to be fully exploited. The basic insight of the radical Left is that although crises are painful and dangerous they are ineluctable, and that they are the terrain on which battles have to be waged and won. The difference between liberalism and the radical Left is that, although they refer to the same three elements (liberal center, populist Right, radical Left), they locate them in a radically different topology: for the liberal center, the radical Left and the Right are two forms of the same "totalitarian" excess; while for the Left, the only true alternative is the one between itself and the liberal mainstream, the populist "radical" Right being nothing but the *symptom* of liberalism's inability to deal with the Leftist threat. When today we hear a politician or an ideologist offering us a choice between liberal freedom and fundamentalist oppression, triumphantly asking (purely rhetorical) questions such as "Do you want women to be excluded from public life and deprived of their elementary rights? Do you want every critic or mocker of religion to be punishable by death?" what should make us suspicious is the very self-evidence of the answer—who would have wanted *that*? The problem is that such a simplistic liberal universalism long ago lost its innocence. This is why, for a true Leftist, the conflict between liberal permissiveness and fundamentalism is ultimately a *false* conflict—a vicious cycle in which two opposed poles generate and presuppose each other. Here one should take an Hegelian step backwards, placing in question the very measure from which fundamentalism appears in all its horror. Liberals have long ago lost their right to judge. What Horkheimer once said should also be applied to today's fundamentalism: those who do not want to talk (critically) about liberal democracy and its noble principles should also keep quiet about religious fundamentalism. And, even more pointedly, one should emphatically insist that the conflict between the State of Israel and the Arabs is a false conflict: even if we will all come to perish because of it, it is a conflict which only mystifies the true issues.

How are we to understand this reversal of an emancipatory thrust into fundamentalist populism? In authentic Marxism, totality is not an ideal, but a critical notion—to locate a phenomenon in its totality does not mean to see the hidden harmony of the Whole, but to include within a system all its "symptoms," it antagonisms and inconsistencies, as integral parts. In this sense then, liberalism and fundamentalism form a "totality," for their opposition is structured so that liberalism itself generates its opposite. Where then do the core values of liberalism—freedom, equality, etc.—stand? The paradox is that liberalism itself is not strong enough to save its own core values from the fundamentalist onslaught. Its problem is that it cannot stand on its own: there is something missing in the liberal edifice. Liberalism is, in its very notion, "parasitic," relying as it does on a presupposed network of communal values that it undermines in the course of its own development. Fundamentalism is a reaction—a false, mystificatory reaction of course—against a real flaw inherent within liberalism, and this is why fundamentalism is, over and again, generated by liberalism. Left to itself, liberalism will slowly undermine itself—the only thing that can save its core is a renewed Left. Or, to put it in the well-known terms of 1968, in order for its key legacy to survive, liberalism will need the brotherly help of the radical Left.

Communism, Again!

In contemporary global capitalism, ideological naturalization has reached an unprecedented level: rare are those who dare even to *dream* utopian dreams about possible alternatives. One after the other, the few surviving communist regimes are re-inventing themselves as the authoritarian protectors of a new, even more dynamic and efficient, "capitalism with Asian values." Far from proving that the era of ideological utopias is behind us, this uncontested hegemony of capitalism is sustained by the properly utopian core of capitalist ideology. Utopias of alternative worlds have been exorcized by the utopia in power, masking itself as pragmatic realism. It is not only the conservative dream of regaining some idealized Past before the Fall, or the image of a bright future as the present universality minus its constitutive obstacle, that is utopian; no less utopian is the liberal-pragmatic idea that one can solve problems gradually, one by one ("people are dying right now in Rwanda, so let's forget about anti-imperialist struggle, let us just prevent the slaughter"; or "one has to fight poverty and racism here and now, not wait for the collapse of the global capitalist order"). John Caputo recently wrote:

> I would be perfectly happy if the far left politicians in the United States were able to reform the system by providing universal health care, effectively redistributing wealth more equitably with a revised IRS code, effectively restricting campaign financing, enfranchising all voters, treating migrant workers humanely, and effecting a multilateral foreign policy that would integrate American power within the international community, etc., i.e., intervene upon capitalism by means of serious

and far-reaching reforms. . . . If after doing all that Badiou and Žižek complained that some Monster called Capital still stalks us, I would be inclined to greet that Monster with a yawn.[55]

The problem here is not Caputo's conclusion that if one can achieve all that within capitalism, why not remain within the system? The problem lies with the "utopian" premise that it is *possible* to achieve all that within the coordinates of global capitalism. What if the particular malfunctionings of capitalism enumerated by Caputo are not merely accidental disturbances but are rather structurally necessary? What if Caputo's dream is a dream of universality (of the universal capitalist order) without its symptoms, without any critical points in which its "repressed truth" articulates itself?

This limitation on reformist gradualism also leads us on to the limits of political cynicism. There is one thing about Henry Kissinger, the ultimate cynical *Realpolitiker*, which cannot but strike all observers: namely, how utterly wrong all his predictions have been. For example, when news reached the West about the anti-Gorbachev military coup of 1991, Kissinger immediately accepted the new regime (which ignominiously collapsed three days later) as a fact—in short, when the socialist regimes were already in a state of living death, he was counting on a long-term pact with them. What this example perfectly demonstrates is the limitation of the cynical attitude: cynics are *les non-dupes qui errent*; what they fail to recognize is the symbolic efficacy of illusions, the way they regulate activity which generates social reality. The position of cynicism is that of popular wisdom—the paradigmatic cynic tells you privately, in a confidential low-key voice: "But don't you get it? That it is all really about [money, power, sex . . .], that all high principles and values are just empty phrases which count for nothing?" In this sense, philosophers effectively "believe in the power of ideas," they believe that "ideas rule the world," and cynics are fully justified in accusing them of

---

55   John Caputo and Gianni Vattimo, *After the Death of God*, New York: Columbia University Press 2007, pp. 124–5.

this sin. What the cynics do not recognize, however, is their own naiveté. It is the philosophers who are the true realists: they are well aware that the cynical position is impossible and inconsistent, that cynics effectively follow the principles they publicly mock. Stalin was a cynic if there ever was one—but precisely as such, he sincerely believed in communism.

After denouncing all the "usual suspects" for utopianism then, perhaps the time has come to focus on the liberal utopia itself. This is how one should answer those who dismiss any attempt to question the fundamentals of the liberal-democratic-capitalist order as being themselves dangerously utopian: what we are confronting in today's crisis are the consequences of the utopian core of this order itself. While liberalism presents itself as anti-utopianism embodied, and the triumph of neoliberalism as a sign that we have left behind the utopian projects responsible for the totalitarian horrors of the twentieth century, it is now becoming clear that the true utopian epoch was that of the happy Clintonite '90s, with its belief that we had reached the "end of history," that humanity had finally found the formula for the optimal socio-economic order. But the experience of recent decades clearly shows that the market is not a benign mechanism which best works when left to its own devices—it requires a good deal of extra-market violence to establish and maintain the conditions for its functioning.

The ongoing financial meltdown demonstrates how difficult it is to disturb the thick undergrowth of utopian premises which determine our acts. As Alain Badiou succinctly put it:

The ordinary citizen must "understand" that it is impossible to make up the shortfall in social security, but that it is imperative to stuff untold billions into the banks' financial hole? We must somberly accept that no one imagines any longer that it's possible to nationalize a factory hounded by competition, a factory employing thousands of workers, but that it is obvious to do so for a bank made penniless by speculation?[56]

56 Alain Badiou, "De quel réel cette crise est-elle le spectacle?" *Le monde*, October 17, 2008.

One should generalize from this statement: although we always recognized the urgency of the problems, when we were fighting AIDS, hunger, water shortages, global warming, and so on, there always seemed to be time to reflect, to postpone decisions (recall how the main conclusion of the last meeting of world leaders in Bali, hailed as a success, was that they would meet again in two years to continue their talks. . .). But with the financial meltdown, the urgency to act was unconditional; sums of an unimaginable magnitude had to be found immediately. Saving endangered species, saving the planet from global warming, saving AIDS patients and those dying for lack of funds for expensive treatments, saving the starving children . . . all this can wait a little bit. The call to "save the banks!" by contrast, is an unconditional imperative which must be met with immediate action. The panic was so absolute that a transnational and non-partisan unity was immediately established, all grudges between world leaders being momentarily forgotten in order to avert *the* catastrophe. But what the much-praised "bi-partisan" approach effectively meant was that even democratic procedures were *de facto* suspended: there was no time to engage in proper debate, and those who opposed the plan in the US Congress were quickly made to fall in with the majority. Bush, McCain and Obama all quickly got together, explaining to confused congressmen and women that there was simply no time for discussion—we were in a state of emergency, and things simply had to be done fast . . . And let us also not forget that the sublimely enormous sums of money were spent not on some clear "real" or concrete problem, but essentially in order to *restore confidence* in the markets, that is, simply to change people's beliefs!

Do we need any further proof that Capital is the Real of our lives, a Real whose imperatives are much more absolute than even the most pressing demands of our social and natural reality? It was Joseph Brodsky who provided an appropriate solution to the search for the mysterious "fifth element," the quintessential ingredient of our reality: "Along with air, earth, water, and fire, money is the fifth natural force a human being has to reckon with most often."[57] If one has any doubts about this, a quick look at the recent financial meltdown should be more than sufficient to dispel them.

Towards the end of 2008, a research group studying trends in tuberculosis epidemics in Eastern Europe over the last few decades made their main results public. Having analyzed data from more than 20 states, the researchers from Cambridge and Yale established a clear correlation between loans made to these states by the IMF and the rise in cases of tuberculosis—once the loans stop, the TB epidemics recede. The explanation for this apparently weird correlation is simple: the condition for getting IMF loans is that the recipient state has to introduce "financial discipline," i.e., reduce public spending; and the first victim of measures destined to reestablish "financial health" is health itself, in other words, spending on public health services. The space then opens up for Western humanitarians to bemoan the catastrophic condition of the medical services in these countries and to offer help in the form of charity.

The financial meltdown made it impossible to ignore the blatant irrationality of global capitalism. Compare the $700 billion spent by the US alone in order to stabilize the banking system to the fact that of the $22 billion pledged by richer nations to help develop poorer nations' agriculture in the face of the current food crisis, only $2.2 billion has so far been made available. The blame for the food crisis cannot be placed on the usual suspects, such as the corruption, inefficiency and state interventionism of Third World states; on the contrary, it is directly dependent on the globalization of agriculture, as none other than Bill Clinton made clear in his comments on the crisis at a UN gathering marking World Food Day, under the indicative title: " 'We Blew It' On Global Food."[58] The gist of Clinton's speech was that the contemporary crisis shows how "we all blew it, including me when I was president," by

---

57   Joseph Brodsky, *Less Than One: Selected Essays*, New York: Farrar Straus and Giroux 1986, p. 157.

58   As reported by Associated Press on October 23, 2008.

treating food crops as commodities rather than as a resource obviously vital to the world's poor. Clinton was very clear in placing the blame not on individual states or governments, but on long-term Western policies imposed by the US and the European Union, and applied for decades by the World Bank, the IMF, and other international institutions. These policies pressured African and Asian countries into dropping government subsidies for fertilizers, improved seed and other farm inputs, thus opening up the way for the best land to be used for export crops and thereby ruining these countries' capacity to be self-sufficient in food production. The result of such "structural adjustments" was the integration of local agriculture into the global economy: as more domestic crops were exported, countries had to rely increasingly on imported food, while farmers thrown off their land were forced into slums, where the only work available was in outsourced sweatshops. In this way, many countries are kept in a state of postcolonial dependence and become increasingly vulnerable to market fluctuations—the skyrocketing of grain prices over the last few years (also caused by the use of crops for biofuel rather than food) has already caused starvation in countries from Haiti to Ethiopia.

In recent years, such strategies have become more systematic and have expanded in scope: major international corporations and governments now look to compensate for shortages of arable land in their own countries by setting up massive industrial farms abroad.[59] For example, in November 2008, Daewoo Logistics in South Korea announced that it had negotiated a 99-year lease on some 3.2 million acres of farmland on Madagascar, amounting to nearly half of its arable land. Daewoo plans to put about three quarters of this land under corn, with the remainder used to produce palm oil, a key commodity in the global biofuels market. But this is just the tip of the iceberg: several European companies have during the past two years taken out leases on land to grow crops for

---

59   See Vivienne Walt, "The breadbasket of South Korea: Madagascar," *Time*, November 23, 2008.

food and biofuels, such as the British company Sun Biofuels, which is planting biofuel crops in Ethiopia, Mozambique, and Tanzania. Africa's fertile soil also appeals to countries in the oil-rich Persian Gulf, whose vast deserts force them to import most of their food. Although such wealthy states are easily able to pay for food imports, the turmoil on the global food markets has only increased their incentive to secure their own sources of supply.

What, then, is the incentive on the other side, for those African countries in which starvation is rife, and whose farmers lack the basic tools, fertilizer, fuel and the transport infrastructure needed to grow crops efficiently and get them to market? The Daewoo representatives claim that their deal will also benefit Madagascar: not only is the land they are leasing not in use now, but,

> although Daewoo plans to export the yield of the land, ... it plans to invest about $6 billion over the next 20 years to build the port facilities, roads, power-plants and irrigation systems necessary to support its agribusiness there, and that will create thousands of jobs for Madagascar's unemployed. Jobs will help the people of Madagascar earn the money to buy their own food—even if it is imported.[60]

The circle of postcolonial dependence is thus closed again, and food-dependency will only be exacerbated.

Are we thus not gradually approaching a global state in which the potential scarcity of three basic material resources (oil, water, and food) will become the determining factor in international politics? Is not the lack of food—which makes itself visible in (for the time being) sporadic crises here and there—one of the signs of the forthcoming apocalypse? While its occurrence is overdetermined by a multitude of factors (growing demand in fast-developing states like India and China; harvest failures due to ecological disturbances; the use of large

---

60 *Ibid.*

parts of arable land in Third World countries for export products; the market-determined use of grains for other purposes such as biofuel), it seems clear that this is not a short-term issue which can be quickly overcome with the appropriate market regulation, but is rather the sign of a long-term problem impossible to solve by means of the market economy. Some apologists for the new world order point out that the lack of food is in itself an indicator of material progress, since people in the fast-developing Third World countries earn more and so can afford to eat more. The problem nonetheless is that this new demand for food pushes millions towards starvation in those countries lacking such fast economic growth.

Does the same not go for the forthcoming energy crisis, and the looming shortages in water supply? In order to approach these problems adequately, it will be necessary to invent new forms of large-scale collective action; neither the standard forms of state intervention nor the much-praised forms of local self-organization will be up to the job. If such problems are not solved one way or another, the most likely scenario will be a new era of apartheid in which secluded parts of the world enjoying an abundance of food, water and energy are separated from a chaotic "outside" characterized by widespread chaos, starvation and permanent war. What should people in Haiti and other regions blighted by food shortages do? Do they not have the full right to violent rebellion? Communism is once again at the gates.

Clinton is right to say that "food is not a commodity like others. We should go back to a policy of maximum food self-sufficiency. It is crazy for us to think we can develop countries around the world without increasing their ability to feed themselves." There are, however, at least two points to add here. First, as was noted earlier with regard to Mali, while imposing the globalization of agriculture on Third World countries, the developed Western countries are taking great care to maintain *their own* food self-sufficiency with financial support for their own farmers, etc. (Recall that financial support to farmers accounts for more than half of the entire European Union budget—the West itself has never abandoned the "policy of maximum food self-sufficiency"!) Second, one should note that the list of products and services which, like food, are not "commodities like others" extends much further, including not only defense (as all "patriots" are aware), but above all water, energy, the environment as such, culture, education, and health . . . Who is to decide on the priorities here, and how, if such decisions cannot be left to the market? It is here that the question of communism has to be raised once again.

2 The Communist Hypothesis

The New Enclosure of the Commons

When, in 1922, after winning the Civil War against all the odds, the Bolsheviks had to retreat into the "New Economic Policy" (NEP), which allowed a much wider scope for the market economy and private property, Lenin wrote a short text entitled "On Ascending a High Mountain." He uses the simile of a climber who has to return to the valley after a first failed attempt to reach a new mountain peak as a way of describing what it means to make a retreat in the revolutionary process. The question is: how does one undertake such a retreat without opportunistically betraying one's fidelity to the Cause? After enumerating both the achievements and the failures of the Soviet state, Lenin concludes: "Communists who have no illusions, who do not give way to despondency, and who preserve their strength and flexibility 'to begin from the beginning' over and over again in approaching an extremely difficult task, are not doomed (and in all probability will not perish)."[1] This is Lenin at his Beckettian best, echoing the line from *Worstward Ho*: "Try again. Fail again. Fail better." His conclusion—"to begin from the beginning over and over again"—makes it clear that he is not talking about merely slowing down progress in order to fortify what has already been achieved, but more radically about *returning to the starting point*: one should "begin from the beginning," not from the peak one may have successfully reached in the previous effort.

---

1 V.I. Lenin, "Notes of a publicist: on ascending a high mountain. . .," in *Collected Works*, Vol. 33, Moscow: Progress Publishers 1965, pp. 204–11.

In Kierkegaardian terms, a revolutionary process involves not a gradual progress, but a repetitive movement, a movement of *repeating the beginning* again and again. And this is exactly where we find ourselves today, after the "obscure disaster" of 1989, the definitive end of the epoch which began with the October Revolution. One should therefore reject any sense of continuity with what the Left meant over the last two centuries. Although sublime moments like the Jacobin climax of the French Revolution and the October Revolution will forever remain a key part of our memory, the general framework has to be surpassed, and everything should be re-thought, beginning from the zero-point. This beginning is, of course, what Badiou calls "the communist hypothesis":

> The communist hypothesis remains the right hypothesis, as I have said, and I do not see any other. If this hypothesis should have to be abandoned, then it is not worth doing anything in the order of collective action. Without the perspective of communism, without this Idea, nothing in the historical and political future is of such a kind as to interest the philosopher. Each individual can pursue their private business, and we won't mention it again. ... But holding on to the Idea, the existence of the hypothesis, does not mean that its first form of presentation, focused on property and the state, must be maintained just as it is. In fact, what we are ascribed as a philosophical task, we could say even a duty, is to help a new modality of existence of the hypothesis to come into being. New in terms of the type of political experimentation to which this hypothesis could give rise.[2]

One should be careful not to read these lines in a Kantian way, conceiving communism as a "regulative Idea," thereby resuscitating the specter of an "ethical socialism" taking equality as its *a priori* norm-axiom. One should rather maintain the precise reference to a set of actual social

---

2   Alain Badiou, *The Meaning of Sarkozy*, London: Verso 2008, p. 115.

antagonisms which generates the need for communism—Marx's notion of communism not as an ideal, but as a movement which reacts to such antagonisms, is still fully relevant. However, if we conceive of communism as an "eternal Idea," this implies that the situation which generates it is no less eternal, i.e., that the antagonism to which communism reacts will always exist. And from here, it is only one small step to a "deconstructive" reading of communism as a dream of presence, of abolishing all alienated re-presentation, a dream which thrives on its own impossibility. How then are we to break out of this formalism in order to formulate antagonisms which will continue to generate the communist Idea? Where are we to look for this Idea's new mode?

It is easy to make fun of Fukuyama's notion of the "End of History," but most people today *are* Fukuyamean, accepting liberal-democratic capitalism as the finally found formula of the best possible society, such that all one can do is to try to make it more just, more tolerant, and so on. A simple but pertinent question arises here: if liberal-democratic capitalism obviously works better than all known alternatives, if liberal-democratic capitalism is, if not the best, then at least the least worst form of society, why do we not simply resign ourselves to it in a mature way, even accept it wholeheartedly? Why insist, against all hope, on the communist idea? Is such an insistence not an exemplary case of the narcissism of the lost cause? And does such narcissism not underlie the predominant attitude of academic Leftists who expect a theoretician to tell them what to do?—they desperately want to commit themselves, but not knowing how to do so effectively, they await the answer from a theoretician. Such an attitude is, of course, in itself false, as if a theory will provide the magic formula, capable of resolving the practical deadlock. The only correct answer here is that if you really do not know what to do, then nobody can tell you, and the cause is irremediably lost.

This deadlock is hardly new—the great defining problem of Western Marxism was the lack of a revolutionary subject or agent. Why is it that the working class does not complete the passage from in-itself to for-itself and constitute itself as a revolutionary agent? This problem was the main motivation for the turn to psychoanalysis, evoked precisely in order to explain the unconscious libidinal mechanisms which were preventing the rise of class consciousness, mechanisms inscribed into the very being (social situation) of the working class. In this way, the truth of Marxist socio-economic analysis could be saved, and there was no need to give ground to "revisionist" theories about the rise of the middle classes. For this same reason, Western Marxism was also engaged in a constant search for other social agents who could play the role of the revolutionary subject, as understudies who might replace the indisposed working class: Third World peasants, students, intellectuals, the excluded . . .

The failure of the working class as a revolutionary subject lies already at the very core of the Bolshevik revolution: Lenin's skill lay in his ability to detect the "rage potential" of the disappointed peasants. The October Revolution took place under the banner of "land and peace," addressed to the vast peasant majority, seizing the brief moment of their radical dissatisfaction. Lenin had already been thinking along these lines a decade earlier, which is why he was so horrified at the prospect of the success of the Stolypin land reforms, aimed at creating a new and stronger class of independent farmers. He was sure that if Stolypin succeeded, the chance for revolution would be lost for decades.

All successful socialist revolutions, from Cuba to Yugoslavia, followed the same model, seizing a local opportunity in an extreme and critical situation, co-opting the desire for national liberation or other forms of "rage capital." Of course, a partisan of the logic of hegemony would here point out that this is the "normal" logic of revolution, that the "critical mass" is reached precisely and only through a series of equivalences among multiple demands, a series which is always radically contingent and dependent on a specific, unique even, set of circumstances. A revolution never occurs when all antagonisms collapse into the Big One, but only when they synergetically combine their power. But the problem is here more complex: the point is not just that revolution no longer rides on the train of History, following its Laws, since there is no History, since history is an open, contingent process. The problem is a different one. It is as if there *is* a Law of History, a more-or-less clear and predominant line of historical development, but that revolution can only occur in its interstices, "against the current." Revolutionaries have to wait patiently for the (usually very brief) moment when the system openly malfunctions or collapses, have to exploit the window of opportunity, to seize power—which at that moment lies, as it were, in the street—and then fortify their hold on it, building up repressive apparatuses, and so forth, so that, once the moment of confusion is over and the majority sobers up only to be disappointed by the new regime, it is too late to reverse things, for the revolutionaries are now firmly entrenched.

The case of communist ex-Yugoslavia is typical here: throughout World War II, the communists ruthlessly hegemonized the resistance against the German occupying forces, monopolizing their role in the anti-fascist struggle by actively seeking to destroy all alternative ("bourgeois") resisting forces, while simultaneously denying the communist nature of their struggle (those who raised the suspicion that the communists planned to grab power and foment a revolution at the end of the war were swiftly denounced as spreading enemy propaganda). After the war, once they did indeed seize full power, things changed quickly and the regime openly displayed its true communist nature. The communists, although genuinely popular until around 1946, nonetheless cheated almost openly in the general election of that year. When asked why they had done so—since they could easily have won in a free election anyway—their answer (in private, of course) was that this was true, but then they would have lost the *next* election four years later, so it was better to make clear now what kind of election they were prepared to tolerate. In short, they were fully aware of the unique opportunity that had brought them to power. An awareness of the communists' historical failure to build and sustain genuine long-term hegemony based on popular support was thus, from the very beginning, taken into account.

Thus again, it is not enough simply to remain faithful to the communist Idea; one has to locate within historical reality antagonisms which give this Idea a practical urgency. The only *true* question today is: do we endorse the predominant naturalization of capitalism, or does today's global capitalism contain antagonisms which are sufficiently strong to prevent its indefinite reproduction? There are four such antagonisms: the looming threat of an *ecological* catastrophe; the inappropriateness of the notion of *private property* in relation to so-called "intellectual property"; the socio-ethical implications of *new techno-scientific developments* (especially in biogenetics); and, last but not least, the creation of *new forms of apartheid*, new Walls and slums. There is a qualitative difference between this last feature—the gap that separates the Excluded from the Included—and the other three, which designate different aspects of what Hardt and Negri call the "commons," the shared substance of our social being, the privatization of which involves violent acts which should, where necessary, be resisted with violent means:

—*the commons of culture*, the immediately socialized forms of "cognitive" capital, primarily language, our means of communication and education, but also the shared infrastructure of public transport, electricity, the postal system, and so on;

—*the commons of external nature*, threatened by pollution and exploitation (from oil to rain forests and the natural habitat itself);

—*the commons of internal nature* (the biogenetic inheritance of humanity); with new biogenetic technology, the creation of a New Man in the literal sense of changing human nature becomes a realistic prospect.

What the struggles in all these domains share is an awareness of the potential for destruction, up to and including the self-annihilation of humanity itself, should the capitalist logic of enclosing the commons be allowed a free run. Nicholas Stern was right to characterize the climate crisis as "the greatest market failure in human history."[3] So when Kishan Khoday, a UN team leader, recently wrote: "There is an increasing spirit of global environmental citizenship, a desire to address climate change

---

3 Quoted from *Time* magazine, December 24, 2007, p. 2.

as a matter of common concern of all humanity,"[4] one should give all weight to the terms "global citizenship" and "common concern"—that is, to the need to establish a global political organization which, neutralizing and channeling market mechanisms, expresses a properly communist perspective.

It is the reference to the "commons" which justifies the resuscitation of the notion of communism: it enables us to see the progressive "enclosure" of the commons as a process of proletarianization of those who are thereby excluded from their own substance. We should certainly not drop the notion of the proletariat, or of the proletarian position; on the contrary, the present conjuncture compels us to radicalize it to an existential level well beyond Marx's imagination. We need a more radical notion of the proletarian subject, a subject reduced to the evanescent point of the Cartesian *cogito*.

For this reason, a new emancipatory politics will stem no longer from a particular social agent, but from an explosive combination of different agents. What unites us is that, in contrast to the classic image of proletariat who have "nothing to lose but their chains," we are in danger of losing *everything*: the threat is that we will be reduced to abstract subjects devoid of all substantial content, dispossessed of our symbolic substance, our genetic base heavily manipulated, vegetating in an unlivable environment. This triple threat to our entire being renders us all proletarians, reduced to "substanceless subjectivity," as Marx put it in the *Grundrisse*. The ethico-political challenge is to recognize ourselves in this figure—in a way, we are all excluded, from nature as well as from our symbolic substance. Today, we are all potentially a *homo sacer*, and the only way to stop that from becoming a reality is to act preventively.

If this sounds apocalyptic, one can only retort that we live in apocalyptic times. It is easy to see how each of the three processes of proletarianization refer to an apocalyptic end point: ecological breakdown, the biogenetic reduction of humans to manipulable machines, total digital control over

---

4   Quoted from ibid.

our lives ... At all these levels, things are approaching a zero-point; "the end of times is near." Here is Ed Ayres's description:

> We are being confronted by something so completely outside our collective experience that we don't really see it, even when the evidence is overwhelming. For us, that "something" is a blitz of enormous biological and physical alterations in the world that has been sustaining us.[5]

At the geological and biological level, Ayres enumerates four "spikes" (accelerated developments) asymptotically approaching a zero-point at which the quantitative expansion will reach a limit and a qualitative change will then occur. The "spikes" are population growth, the consumption of finite resources, carbon gas emissions, and the mass extinction of species. In order to cope with these threats, the dominant ideology is mobilizing mechanisms of dissimulation and self-deception which include a will to ignorance: "a general pattern of behavior among threatened human societies is to become more blinkered, rather than more focused on the crisis, as they fail." The same goes for the ongoing economic crisis: in late Spring 2009 it was successfully "renormalized"—the panic blew over, the situation was proclaimed as "getting better," or at least the damage as having been controlled (the price paid for this "recovery" in the Third World countries was, of course, rarely mentioned)—thereby constituting an ominous warning that the true message of the crisis had been ignored, and that we could relax once again and continue our long march towards the apocalypse.

Apocalypse is characterized by a specific mode of time, clearly opposed to the two other predominant modes: traditional circular time (time ordered and regulated on cosmic principles, reflecting the order of nature and the heavens; the time-form in which microcosm and macrocosm resonate in harmony), and the modern linear time of

---

5   Ed Ayres, "Why are we not astonished," *World Watch*, Vol. 12, May 1999.

gradual progress or development. Apocalyptic time is the "time of the end of time," the time of emergency, of the "state of exception" when the end is nigh and we can only prepare for it. There are at least four different versions of apocalyptism today: Christian fundamentalism, New Age spirituality, techno-digital post-humanism, and secular ecologism. Although they all share the basic notion that humanity is approaching a zero-point of radical transmutation, their respective ontologies differ radically: Techno-digital apocalyptism (of which Ray Kurzweil is the main representative) remains within the confines of scientific naturalism, and discerns in the evolution of human species the contours of our transformation into "post-humans." New Age spirituality gives this transmutation a further twist, interpreting it as the shift from one mode of "cosmic awareness" to another (usually a shift from the modern dualist-mechanistic stance to one of holistic immersion). Christian fundamentalists of course read the apocalypse in strictly biblical terms, that is, they search for (and find) in the contemporary world signs that the final battle between Christ and the Anti-Christ is imminent. Finally, secular ecologism shares the naturalist stance of post-humanism, but gives it a negative twist—what lies ahead, the "omega point" we are approaching, is not a progression to a higher "post-human" level, but the catastrophic self-destruction of humanity. Although Christian funda-mentalist apocalyptism is considered the most ridiculous, and dangerous, in its content, it remains the version closest to a radical "millenarian" emancipatory logic. The task is thus to bring it into closer contact with secular ecologism, thereby conceiving the threat of annihilation as the chance for a radical emancipatory renewal.

Socialism or Communism?

Such apocalyptic proletarianization is, however, inadequate if we want to deserve the name of "communist." The ongoing enclosure of the commons concerns both the relation of people to the objective conditions of their life processes as well as the relation between people themselves: the commons are privatized at the expense of the proletarianized majority. But there is a gap between these two kinds of relation: the commons can also be restored to collective humanity without communism, in an authoritarian-communitarian regime; likewise the de-substantialized, "rootless" subject, deprived of content, can also be counteracted in ways that tend in the direction of communitarianism, with the subject finding its proper place in a new substantial community. In this precise sense, Negri's anti-socialist title, *GoodBye Mr. Socialism*, was correct: communism is to be opposed to socialism, which, in place of the egalitarian collective, offers an organic community (Nazism was national socialism, not national communism). In other words, while there may be a socialist anti-Semitism, there cannot be a communist form. (If it appears otherwise, as in Stalin's last years, it is only as an indicator of a lack of fidelity to the revolutionary event.) Eric Hobsbawm recently published a column with the title: "Socialism Failed, Capitalism Is Bankrupt. What Comes Next?" The answer is: communism. Socialism wants to solve the first three antagonisms without addressing the fourth—without the singular universality of the proletariat. The only way for the global capitalist system to survive its long-term antagonism and simultaneously avoid the communist solution, will be for it to reinvent some kind of socialism—in the guise of communitarianism, or populism, or capitalism with Asian values, or some other configuration. The future will thus be communist . . . or socialist.

As Michael Hardt has put it, if capitalism stands for private property and socialism for state property, communism stands for the overcoming of property as such in the commons.[6] Socialism is what Marx called "vulgar communism," in which we get only what Hegel would have called the abstract negation of property, that is, the negation of property within the field of property—it is "universalized private property." Hence the title of the *Newsweek* cover story of February 16, 2009: "We are all socialists now," and its subtitle, "In many ways our economy already resembles a

---

6 In his intervention at the conference "The Idea of Communism," Birkbeck College, London, March 13–15, 2009.

European one," is fully justified, if properly understood: even in the US, the bastion of economic liberalism, capitalism is having to re-invent socialism in order to save itself.[7] The irony of the fact that this process of coming to "resemble Europe" is further characterized by the prediction that "we [in the US] will become even more French" cannot but strike the reader. After all, Sarkozy was elected as French president on a platform of finally finishing off the tradition of European welfare-state socialism and rejoining the Anglo-Saxon liberal model—and yet the very model he proposed to imitate is now returning to just what he wanted to move away from: the allegedly discredited path of large-scale state intervention in the economy. The much-maligned European "social model," decried as inefficient and out of date under the conditions of postmodern capitalism, has tasted its revenge. But there is no reason for joy here: socialism is no longer to be conceived as the infamous "lower phase" of communism, it is its true competitor, the greatest threat to it. (Perhaps the time has come to remember that throughout the twentieth century social democracy was an instrument mobilized to counteract the communist threat to capitalism.) Thus the completion of Negri's title should be: *GoodBye Mr. Socialism . . . and Welcome, Comrade Communism!*

What the communist fidelity to the proletarian position involves is thus an unambiguous rejection of any ideology implying a return to any kind of prelapsarian substantial unity. On November 28, 2008, Evo Morales, the president of Bolivia, issued a public letter on the subject "Climate Change: Save the Planet from Capitalism." Here are its opening statements:

Sisters and brothers: Today, our Mother Earth is ill. . . . Everything began with the industrial revolution in 1750, which gave birth to the capitalist system. In two and a half centuries, the so called "developed" countries have consumed a large part of the fossil fuels created over five million centuries. . . . Competition and the thirst for profit without limits of the

---

7   Jon Meacham and Evan Thomas, "We are all socialists now," *Newsweek*, February 16, 2009.

capitalist system are destroying the planet. Under Capitalism we are not human beings but consumers. Under Capitalism Mother Earth does not exist, instead there are raw materials. Capitalism is the source of the asymmetries and imbalances in the world.[8]

The politics pursued by the Morales government in Bolivia is on the very cutting edge of contemporary progressive struggle. Nonetheless, the lines just quoted demonstrate with painful clarity its ideological limitations (for which one always pays a practical price). Morales relies in a simplistic way on the narrative of the Fall which took place at a precise historical moment: "Everything began with the industrial revolution in 1750 . . ."—and, predictably, this Fall consists in losing our roots in mother earth: "Under Capitalism mother earth does not exist." (To this, one is tempted to add that, if there is one good thing about capitalism, it is that, precisely, mother earth now no longer exists.) "Capitalism is the source of the asymmetries and imbalances in the world"—meaning that our goal should be to restore a "natural" balance and symmetry. What is thereby attacked and rejected is the very process that gave rise to modern subjectivity and that obliterates the traditional sexualized cosmology of mother earth (and father heaven), along with the idea that our roots lie in the substantial "maternal" order of nature.

Fidelity to the communist Idea thus means that, to repeat Arthur Rimbaud, *il faut être absolument moderne*—we should remain resolutely modern and reject the all too glib generalization whereby the critique of capitalism morphs into the critique of "instrumental reason" or "modern technological civilization." This is why we should insist on the qualitative difference between the fourth antagonism—the gap that separates the Excluded from the Included—and the other three: it is only this reference to the Excluded that justifies the use of the term communism. There is nothing more "private" than a state community which perceives the Excluded as a threat and worries how to keep them at a proper distance.

---

8   Evo Morales, "Climate change: save the planet from capitalism," available online at *http://climateandcapitalism.com*.

In the series of the four antagonisms then, that between the Included and the Excluded is the crucial one. Without it, all others lose their subversive edge—ecology turns into a problem of sustainable development, intellectual property into a complex legal challenge, biogenetics into an ethical issue. One can sincerely fight to preserve the environment, defend a broader notion of intellectual property, or oppose the copyrighting of genes, without ever confronting the antagonism between the Included and the Excluded. Furthermore, one can even formulate certain aspects of these struggles in the terms of the Included being threatened by the polluting Excluded. In this way, we get no true universality, only "private" concerns in the Kantian sense of the term. Corporations such as Whole Foods and Starbucks continue to enjoy favor among liberals even though they both engage in anti-union activities; the trick is that they sell their products with a progressive spin. One buys coffee made with beans bought at above fair-market value, one drives a hybrid vehicle, one buys from companies that ensure good benefits for their staff and customers (according to the corporation's own standards), and so on. In short, without the antagonism between the Included and the Excluded, we may well find ourselves in a world in which Bill Gates is the greatest humanitarian battling against poverty and disease, and Rupert Murdoch the greatest environmentalist mobilizing hundreds of millions through his media empire.

There is another key difference between the first three antagonisms and the fourth: the first three effectively concern questions of the (economic, anthropological, even physical) *survival* of humanity, but the fourth is ultimately a question of *justice*. If humanity does not resolve its ecological predicament, we may all vanish; but one can well imagine a society which somehow resolves the first three antagonisms through authoritarian measures which not only maintain but in fact strengthen existing social hierarchies, divisions and exclusions. In Lacanese, we are dealing here with the gap that separates the series of ordinary signifiers (S_2) from the Master-Signifier (S_1), that is, with a struggle for hegemony: which pole in the antagonism between the

Included and the Excluded will "hegemonize" the other three? One can no longer rely on the old Marxist logic of "historical necessity" which claims that the first three problems will only be solved if one wins the key "class" struggle between the Excluded and the Included—the logic of "only the overcoming of class distinctions can really resolve our ecological predicament." There is a common feature shared by all four antagonisms: the process of proletarianization, of the reduction of human agents to pure subjects deprived of their substance; this proletarianization, however, works in different ways. In the first three cases, it deprives agents of their substantial content; in the fourth case, it is the formal fact of excluding certain figures from socio-political space. We should underline this structure of 3 + 1, namely the reflection of the external tension between subject and substance ("man" deprived of its substance) within the human collective. There are subjects who, within the human collective, directly embody the proletarian position of substanceless subjectivity. Which is why the Communist wager is that the only way to solve the "external" problem (the re-appropriation of alienated substance) is to radically transform the inner-subjective (social) relations.

It is thus crucial to insist on the communist-egalitarian emancipatory Idea, and insist on it in a very precise Marxian sense: there are social groups which, on account of their lacking a determinate place in the "private" order of the social hierarchy, stand directly for universality; they are what Rancière calls the "part of no-part" of the social body. All truly emancipatory politics is generated by the short-circuit between the universality of the "public use of reason" and the universality of the "part of no-part"—this was already the communist dream of the young Marx: to bring together the universality of philosophy with the universality of the proletariat. From Ancient Greece, we have a name for the intrusion of the Excluded into the socio-political space: democracy. Our question today is whether democracy is still an appropriate name for this egalitarian explosion. Two extreme positions here are, on the one hand, the cursory dismissal of democracy as the mere illusory form of appearance of its opposite (class domination), and on the other the claim that the democracy we have, really existing democracy, is a distortion of true democracy—along the lines of Gandhi's famous reply to the British journalist who asked him about Western civilization: "A good idea. Perhaps we should put it into practice!" Obviously, the debate which moves between these two extremes is too abstract: what we need to address is the question of how democracy relates to the dimension of universality embodied in the Excluded.

This focus on the walls that separate the Excluded from the Included may easily be misunderstood as a clandestine return to the liberal-tolerant-multicultural topic of "openness" ("no one should be left out, all minority groups, lifestyles, etc., should be allowed in") at the expense of a properly Marxist notion of social antagonism. It might also be criticized from the opposite "postmodern" perspective as marking a theoretical regression to a naive Excluded/Included opposition that ignores the complex "micro-political" apparatus of social control and regulation analyzed by Foucault. Peter Hallward makes a similar critical point in response to Badiou's notion of invisibility, of "counting-for-nothing," of the symptomal element of the social edifice (Rancière's "part of no-part"):

Practical political work is more often concerned with people or situations who are not so much invisible or unseen as under-seen or mis-seen; they do not count for nothing so much as for very little. They are not simply excluded so much as oppressed and exploited. This difference involves more than nuance. As several generations of emancipatory thinkers have now argued, modern forms of power do not primarily exclude or prohibit but rather modulate, guide or enhance the behaviour and norms conducive to the status quo; the model of power that seems tacitly to inform Badiou's recent work, by contrast, still seems to pre-date Foucault, if not Gramsci.[9]

---

9   Peter Hallward, "Order and event," *New Left Review* 53 (September–October 2008), p. 104.

In this choice of "Badiou versus Foucault," one should nonetheless insist on a dimension ignored by the Foucauldian approach, a dimension on which Badiou's notion of invisibility focuses. That is to say, in the Foucauldian notion of productive power, a power which works not in an exclusionary way, but in an enabling/regulatory way, there is no room for Badiou's notion of the point of inconsistency (or the "symptomal torsion") of a situation, that element of a situation for which there is no proper place (with)in the situation—not for accidental reasons but because its dislocation/exclusion is constitutive of the situation itself. Take the case of the proletariat: of course, the working class is "visible" in multiple ways within the capitalist world (as those who freely sell their labor-power on the market; as a potential rabble; as faithful and disciplined servants of capitalist managers, etc.). However, none of these modes of visibility covers up the symptomal role of the proletariat as the "part of no-part" of the capitalist universe. Badiou's "invisibility" is thus the obverse of visibility within the hegemonic ideological space, it is what has to remain invisible so that the visible may be visible. Or, to put it in another, more traditional, way: what the Foucauldian approach cannot grasp is the notion of a two-faced symptomal element, whose one face is a marginal accident of a situation, and whose other face is (to stand for) the truth of this same situation. In the same way, the "excluded" are, of course, visible, in the precise sense that, paradoxically, *their exclusion itself is the mode of their inclusion*: their "proper place" in the social body is that of exclusion (from the public sphere).

This is why Lacan claimed that Marx had already invented the (Freudian) notion of a symptom: for both Marx and Freud, the way to the truth of a system (of society, of the psyche) leads through what necessarily appears as a "pathological" marginal and accidental distortion of this system: slips of tongue, dreams, symptoms, economic crises. The Freudian Unconscious is thus "invisible" in an exactly homologous way, which is why there is no place for it in Foucault's edifice. This is why Foucault's rejection of what he calls the Freudian "repression hypothesis"—his notion of regulatory power discourses which generate sexuality in the very act of describing and regulating it—misses the (Freudian) point. Freud and Lacan were well aware that there is no repression without the return of the repressed, they were well aware that the repressive discourse generates what it represses. However, what this discourse represses is not what it appears to repress, not what it itself takes to be the threatening X it seeks to control. The figures of "sexuality" it portrays as the threat to be controlled—such as the figure of the Woman, whose uncontrolled sexuality is a threat to the masculine order—are themselves fantasmatic mystifications. Rather, what this discourse "represses" is (among other things) its own contamination by what it tries to control—say, the way the sacrifice of sexuality sexualizes sacrifice itself, or the manner in which the effort to control sexuality sexualizes this controlling activity itself. Sexuality is thus, of course, not "invisible"—it is controlled and regulated. What is "invisible" is the sexualization of this very work of control: not the elusive object we try to control, but the mode of our own participation within it.

Liberals who acknowledge the problems of those excluded from the socio-political process formulate their goal as being the inclusion of those whose voices are not heard: all positions should be listened to, all interests taken into account, the human rights of everyone guaranteed, all ways of life, cultures and practises respected, and so on. The obsession of this democratic discourse is the protection of all kinds of minorities: cultural, religious, sexual, *e tutti quanti*. The formula of democracy is patient negotiation and compromise. What gets lost here is the proletarian position, the position of universality embodied in the Excluded. This is why, upon a closer look, it becomes clear that what Hugo Chávez has begun doing in Venezuela differs markedly from the standard liberal form of inclusion: Chávez is not including the excluded in a pre-existing liberal-democratic framework; he is, on the contrary, taking the "excluded" dwellers of favelas as his *base* and then reorganizing political space and political forms of organization so that the latter will "fit" the excluded. Pedantic and abstract as it may appear, this difference—between "bourgeois democracy" and "dictatorship of the proletariat"—is crucial.

A century ago, Vilfredo Pareto was the first to describe the so-called

80/20 rule of social (and not only social) life: 80 percent of land is owned by 20 percent of the people, 80 percent of profits are produced by 20 percent of the employees, 80 percent of decisions are made during 20 percent of meeting time, 80 percent of the links on the Web point to less than 20 percent of Webpages, 80 percent of peas come from 20 percent of the peapods. As some social analysts and economists have suggested, the contemporary explosion of economic productivity confronts us with the ultimate case of this rule: the coming global economy will tend towards a state in which only 20 percent of the labor force are able to do all the necessary work, so that 80 percent of people will be basically irrelevant and of no use, thus potentially unemployed. As this logic reaches its extreme, would it not be reasonable to bring it to its self-negation: is not a system which renders 80 percent of people irrelevant and useless *itself irrelevant and of no use*?

Toni Negri once gave an interview to *Le Monde* during which, strolling along a suburban street in Venezia-Mestre with the journalist, he came across a line of workers picketing outside a textile factory. Pointing to the workers he dismissively remarked: "It's crazy, it's like a Fellini film!"[10] For Negri, the workers stood for all that is wrong with traditional trade-unionist socialism focused on corporate job security, a socialism mercilessly rendered obsolete by the dynamics of "postmodern" capitalism and the hegemonic position of cognitive labor. According to Negri, instead of reacting to this "new spirit of capitalism" in the traditional social-democratic fashion, seeing it as a threat, one should fully embrace it, in order to discern within it—in the dynamics of cognitive labor with its non-hierarchical and non-centralized forms of social interaction—the seeds of communism. But if we follow this logic to the end, it becomes hard not to agree with the cynical neoliberal argument that, today, the main task of the trade unions should be that of re-training workers for absorption into the new digitalized economy.

But what about the opposite vision? Insofar as the dynamic of the new

---

10   "Nous sommes déjà des hommes nouveaux," *Le Monde*, July 13, 2007.

capitalism is rendering an ever greater percentage of workers superfluous, what about the project of reuniting the "living dead" of global capitalism, all those left behind by neo-capitalist "progress," all those rendered useless and obsolete, all those unable to adapt to the new conditions? The wager is, of course, that one might enact a direct short-circuit between these left-overs of history and history's most progressive aspect.

The "Public Use of Reason"

This brings us to the next elementary definition of communism: in contrast to socialism, communism refers to singular universality, to the direct link between the singular and the universal, bypassing particular determinations. When Paul says that, from a Christian standpoint, "there are no men or women, no Jews or Greeks," he thereby claims that ethnic roots, national identities, etc., are *not a category of truth*. To put it in precise Kantian terms: when we reflect upon our ethnic roots, we engage in a *private use of reason*, constrained by contingent dogmatic presuppositions; that is, we act as "immature" individuals, not as free humans who dwell in the dimension of the universality of reason. The opposition between Kant and Rorty with regard to this distinction of public and private is rarely noted, but is nonetheless crucial. Both sharply distinguish between the two domains, but in opposite ways. For Rorty, the great contemporary liberal *par excellence*, the private is the space of our idiosyncrasies where creativity and wild imagination rule and moral considerations are (almost) suspended; the public, on the contrary, is the space of social interaction where we are obliged to obey the rules in order not to hurt others. In Rorty's own terms, the private is the space of irony, while the public is the space of solidarity. For Kant, however, the public space of the "world-civil-society" exemplifies the paradox of universal singularity, of a singular subject who, in a kind of short-circuit, bypassing the mediation of the particular, directly participates in the Universal. This then is what Kant, in a famous passage from his essay "What is Enlightenment?" means by "public" as opposed to "private": "private" designates not one's individual as opposed to communal ties, but the very communal-institutional order of one's particular identification; while "public" refers to the transnational universality of the exercise of one's Reason:

> The public use of one's reason must always be free, and it alone can bring about enlightenment among men. The private use of one's reason, on the other hand, may often be very narrowly restricted without particularly hindering the progress of enlightenment. By public use of one's reason I understand the use which a person makes of it as a scholar before the reading public. Private use I call that which one may make of it in a particular civil post or office which is entrusted to him.[11]

The paradox of Kant's formula "Think freely, but obey!" (which, of course, poses a series of problems of its own, since it also relies on the distinction between the "performative" level of social authority and the level of free thinking where performativity is suspended) is thus that one participates in the universal dimension of the "public" sphere precisely as a singular individual extracted from, or even opposed to, one's substantial communal identification—one is truly universal only when radically singular, in the interstices of communal identities. It is Kant who should be read here as the critic of Rorty. In his vision of public space characterized by the unconstrained exercise of Reason, he invokes a dimension of emancipatory universality *outside* the confines of one's social identity, of one's position within the order of (social) being—precisely the dimension so crucially missing in Rorty.

This space of singular universality is what, within Christianity, appears as the "Holy Spirit"—the space of a collective of believers *subtracted* from the field of organic communities, or of particular life-worlds ("neither Greeks nor Jews"). Consequently, is Kant's "Think freely, but obey!" not a new version of Christ's "Render therefore unto

---

11   Immanuel Kant, "What is Enlightenment?" in Isaac Kramnick (ed.), *The Portable Enlightenment Reader*, New York: Penguin Books 1995, p. 5.

Caesar the things which are Caesar's; and unto God the things that are God's"? "Render unto Caesar the things which are Caesar's": in other words, respect and obey the "private" particular life-world of your community; "and unto God the things that are God's": in other words, participate in the universal space of the community of believers. The Paulinian collective of believers is a proto-model of the Kantian "world-civil-society," and the domain of the state itself is thus in its own way "private": private in the precise Kantian sense of the "private use of Reason" in the State administrative and ideological apparatuses.

In his later *Conflict of Faculties*, Kant prolongs these reflections in addressing a simple but hard-to-answer question: is there true progress in history? (He meant ethical progress, not just material development.) He conceded that actual history is confused and allows for no clear proof on the matter (think for example of how the twentieth century brought an unprecedented expansion of democracy and welfare provision, but also the Holocaust and the Gulag . . .), but he nonetheless concluded that, although progress cannot be proven, we can discern signs which do indicate that it is possible. Kant interpreted the French Revolution as one such sign, which pointed towards the possibility of freedom: the hitherto unthinkable happened, a whole people had fearlessly asserted its freedom and equality. For Kant, even more important than the often bloody reality of the events in the streets of Paris was the enthusiasm those events gave rise to in the eyes of sympathetic observers all around Europe:

> The recent Revolution of a people which is rich in spirit, may well either fail or succeed, accumulate misery and atrocity, it nevertheless arouses in the heart of all spectators (who are not themselves caught up in it) a taking of sides according to desires which borders on enthusiasm and which, since its very expression was not without danger, can only have been caused by a moral disposition within the human race.[12]

---

12   Immanuel Kant, "The conflict of faculties," in *Political Writings*, Cambridge:

One should note here that the French Revolution generated enthusiasm not only in Europe, but also in faraway places such as Haiti. The enthusiasm felt there was not just that of the Kantian spectator, but took an engaged, practical form at a key moment in another world-historical event: the first revolt of black slaves fighting for full participation in the emancipatory project of the French Revolution.

Obama's electoral victory in the US belongs, at a certain level, to the same line. One can and should entertain cynical doubts about the real consequences of Obama's victory: from a pragmatic-realistic perspective, it is quite possible that Obama will turn out to be a "Bush with a human face," making no more than a few minor face-lifting improvements. He will pursue the same basic politics in a more attractive mode and thus possibly even strengthen US hegemony, damaged as it has been by the catastrophe of the Bush years. There is nonetheless something deeply wrong in such a reaction—a key dimension is missing. It is in light of the Kantian conception of enthusiasm that Obama's victory should be viewed not simply as another shift in the eternal parliamentary struggle for a majority, with all its pragmatic calculations and manipulations. It is a sign of something more. This is why a good American friend of mine, a hardened Leftist with no illusions, cried for hours when the news came through of Obama's victory. Whatever our doubts, fears and compromises, for that instant of enthusiasm, each of us was free and participating in the universal freedom of humanity.

The reason Obama's victory generated such enthusiasm was not only the fact that, against all the odds, it really happened, but that the *possibility* of such a thing happening was demonstrated. The same goes for all great historical ruptures—recall the fall of the Berlin Wall. Although we all knew about the rotten inefficiency of the communist regimes, we somehow did not "really believe" that they would disintegrate—like Henry Kissinger, we were all too much victims of a cynical pragmatism. This attitude is best encapsulated by the French expression

Cambridge University Press 1991, p. 182.

je sais bien, mais quand même—I know very well that it can happen, but all the same (I cannot really accept that it will happen). This is why, although Obama's victory was clearly predictable, at least for the last two weeks before the election, his actual victory was still experienced as a surprise—in some sense, the unthinkable had happened, something which we really did not believe *could* happen. (Note that there is also a tragic version of the unthinkable really taking place: the Holocaust, the Gulag . . . how can one accept that something like that could happen?)

This is also how one should answer those who point to all the compromises Obama had to make to become electable. The danger Obama courted in his campaign is that he was already applying to himself what the later historical censorship applied to Martin Luther King, namely, cleansing his program of contentious topics in order to assure his eligibility. There is a famous dialogue in Monty Python's religious spoof *The Life of Brian*, set in Palestine at the time of Christ: the leader of a Jewish revolutionary resistance organization passionately argues that the Romans have brought only misery to the Jews; when his followers remark that they have nonetheless introduced education, built roads, constructed irrigation, and so on, he triumphantly concludes: "All right, but apart from the sanitation, education, medicine, wine, public order, irrigation, roads, the fresh-water system and public health, what have the Romans ever done for us?" Do the latest proclamations by Obama not follow the same line? "I stand for a radical break with Bush's politics! OK, I pleaded for full support for Israel, for continuing the war on terror in Afghanistan and Pakistan, for refusing prosecutions against those who ordered torture, and so on, but I still stand for a radical break with Bush's politics!" Obama's inauguration speech concluded this process of "political self-cleansing"—which is why it was such a disappointment even for many left-liberals in the US. It was a well-crafted but weirdly anemic speech whose message to "all other peoples and governments who are watching today" was: "we are ready to lead once more"; "we will not apologize for our way of life, nor will we waver in its defense."

During the election campaign, it was often noted that when Obama talked about the "audacity of hope," about a change we can believe in, he relied on a rhetoric which lacked any specific content: to hope for what? To change what? Now things are a little clearer: Obama proposes a tactical change destined to reassert the fundamental goals of US politics: the defense of the American way of life and a leading role internationally for the US. The US empire will be now more humane, and respectful of others; it will lead through dialogue, rather than through the brutal imposition of its will. If the Bush administration was the empire with a brutal face, now we shall have the empire with a human face—but it will be the same empire. In Obama's June 2009 speech in Cairo, in which he tried to reach out to the Muslim world, he formulated the debate in terms of the depoliticized dialogue of religions (not even of civilizations)—this was Obama at his politically-correct worst.

Nevertheless, such a pessimistic view falls short. The global situation is not only a harsh reality, it is also defined by its ideological contours, by what is visible and invisible within it, sayable and unsayable. Recall Ehud Barak's response to Gideon Levy for *Ha'aretz*, more than a decade ago, when he was asked what he would have done had he been born a Palestinian: "I would have joined a terrorist organization." This statement had nothing whatsoever to do with endorsing terrorism—but it had everything to do with opening a space for a dialogue with the Palestinians. Remember Gorbachev launching the slogans of *glasnost* and *perestroika*—no matter how he "really meant" them, he unleashed an avalanche which changed the world. Or, to take a negative example: today, even those who oppose torture accept it as a topic of public debate—a major regression in our common discourse. Words are never "only words"; they matter because they define the contours of what we can do.

In this respect then, Obama has already demonstrated an extraordinary ability to change the limits of what one can say publicly. His greatest achievement up to now is that, in his refined non-provocative way, he has introduced into public speech topics which had hitherto been *de facto* unsayable: the continuing importance of race in politics, the positive role of atheists in public life, the necessity to talk with "enemies" like Iran or Hamas, and so on. This is just what US politics needs today more than anything, if it is to break out of its gridlock: new words which will change the way we think and act.

Many of Obama's acts as president also already point in this direction (his educational and healthcare plans, his overtures to Cuba and other "rogue" states, for example). However, as already noted, the real tragedy of Obama is that he has every chance of turning out to be the ultimate savior of capitalism and, as such, one of the great conservative American presidents. There are progressive things that only a conservative with the right hard-line patriotic credentials can do: only de Gaulle was able to grant independence to Algeria; only Nixon was able to establish relations with China—in both cases, had a progressive president done these things, he would have been instantly accused of betraying national interests, selling out to the communists or to terrorists, and so on. Obama's predicament seems to be exactly the opposite one: his "progressive" credentials are enabling him to enforce the "structural readjustments" necessary to stabilize the system.

Nevertheless, these consequences, inevitable as they may prove to be, in no way devalue the authentic Kantian enthusiasm triggered by Obama's victory. The latter was a sign of history in the triple Kantian sense of *signum rememorativum, demonstrativum, prognosticum*: a sign in which the memory of the long *past* of slavery and the struggle for its abolition reverberates; an event which demonstrates a change right *now*; and a hope for *future* achievements. No wonder Obama's victory gave birth to this same universal enthusiasm all around the world, with people dancing on the streets from Berlin to Rio de Janeiro. All the scepticism displayed behind closed doors, even by many worried progressives (what if, in the privacy of the voting booth, the publicly disavowed racism were to re-emerge?), was disproved.

... in Haiti

All this, however, is still insufficient if we want to talk about communism. What then is missing here, in such Kantian enthusiasm? To approach the answer, one must turn to Hegel, who fully shared Kant's enthusiasm in his own description of the impact of the French Revolution:

> This was accordingly a glorious mental dawn. All thinking beings shared in the jubilation of this epoch. Emotions of a lofty character stirred men's minds at that time; a spiritual enthusiasm thrilled through the world, as if the reconciliation between the divine and the secular was now first accomplished.[13]

But he added something crucial, implicitly at least. As Susan Buck-Morss has demonstrated in her essay "Hegel and Haiti,"[14] the successful slave uprising in Haiti, which resulted in the free Haitian republic, was the silent—and, for that reason, all the more effective—point of reference for (or the absent Cause of) Hegel's dialectic of Master and Slave, first introduced in his Jena manuscripts and developed further in his *Phenomenology of Spirit*. Buck-Morss's simple statement "there is no doubt that Hegel and Haiti belong together" concisely captures the explosive result of the short-circuit between these two heterogeneous terms.[15] "Hegel and Haiti"—this is also, perhaps, the most succinct formula of communism.

As Louis Sala-Molins has put it with acerbic brutality: "European Enlightenment philosophers railed against slavery, *except where it literally existed.*"[16] Although they complained that people were (metaphorically speaking) "slaves" of the tyrannical royal powers, they ignored the *literal* slavery that was exploding in scale in the colonies, excusing it on culturalist-racist grounds. When, echoing the French

---

13   G.F.W. Hegel, *The Philosophy of History*, New York: Dover 1956.

14   First published in 2000 as an essay in *Critical Inquiry*, then expanded into a book: *Hegel, Haiti, and Universal History*, Pittsburgh: University of Pittsburgh Press 2009.

15   *Hegel, Haiti, and Universal History*, p. 20

16   Ibid., p. 149.

Revolution, the black slaves in Haiti revolted in the name of the same principles of freedom, equality, and fraternity, this was "the crucible, the trial by fire for the ideals of the French Enlightenment. And every European who was part of the bourgeois reading public knew it. 'The eyes of the world are now on St. Domingo.' "[17] In Haiti, the unthinkable (for the European Enlightenment) took place: the Haitian Revolution "entered history with the peculiar characteristic of being unthinkable even as it happened."[18] The ex-slaves of Haiti took the French revolutionary slogans more literally than did the French themselves: they ignored all the implicit qualifications which abounded in Enlightenment ideology (freedom—but only for rational "mature" subjects, not for the wild immature barbarians who first had to undergo a long process of education in order to deserve freedom and equality . . .). This led to sublime "communist" moments, like the one that occurred when French soldiers (sent by Napoleon to suppress the rebellion and restore slavery) approached the black army of (self-)liberated slaves. When they heard an initially indistinct murmur coming from the black crowd, the soldiers at first assumed it must be some kind of tribal war chant; but as they came closer, they realized that the Haitians were singing the *Marseillaise*, and they started to wonder out loud whether they were not fighting on the wrong side. Events such as these enact universality as a political category. In them, as Buck-Morss put it, "universal humanity is visible at the edges":[19]

> rather than giving multiple, distinct cultures equal due, whereby people are recognized as part of humanity indirectly through the mediation of collective cultural identities, human universality emerges in the historical event at the point of rupture. It is in the discontinuities of history that people whose culture has been strained to the breaking point give expression to a humanity that goes beyond cultural limits.

17   Ibid., p. 42.
18   Michel-Rolph Trouillot, quoted in ibid. p. 50.
19   Ibid., p. 151.

And it is in our emphatic identification with this raw, free, and vulnerable state, that we have a chance of understanding what they say. Common humanity exists in spite of culture and its differences. A person's nonidentity with the collective allows for subterranean solidarities that have a chance of appealing to universal, moral sentiment, the source today of enthusiasm and hope.[20]

Buck-Morss provides here a precise argument against the postmodern poetry of diversity: the latter masks the underlying *sameness* of the brutal violence enacted by culturally diverse cultures and regimes: "Can we rest satisfied with the call for acknowledging 'multiple modernities,' with a politics of 'diversity,' or 'multiversality,' when in fact the inhumanities of these multiplicities are often strikingly the same?"[21] But, one may ask, was the ex-slaves' singing of the *Marseillaise* ultimately not an index of colonialist subordination—even in their self-liberation, did not the Blacks have to follow the emancipatory model of the colonial metropolis? And is this not similar to the idea that contemporary opponents of US politics should be singing the *Stars and Stripes*? Surely the true revolutionary act would have been for the colonizers to sing the songs of the colonized? The mistake in this reproach is double. First, contrary to appearances, it is far more acceptable for the colonial power to see its own people singing others' (the colonized's) songs than songs which express their own identity—as a sign of tolerance and patronizing respect, colonizers love to learn and sing the songs of the colonized. . . Second, and much more importantly, the message of the Haitian soldiers' *Marseillaise* was not "You see, even we, the primitive blacks, are able to assimilate ourselves to your high culture and politics, to imitate it as a model!" but a much more precise one: "in this battle, we are more French than you, the Frenchmen, are—we stand for the innermost consequences of your revolutionary ideology, the very consequences you were not able to assume." Such a message cannot but be deeply unsettling for the

---

20 Ibid., p. 133.
21 Ibid., p. 138–9.

colonizers—and it would certainly not be the message of those who, today, might sing the *Stars and Stripes* when confronting the US army. (Although, as a thought experiment, if we imagine a situation in which this *could* be the message, there would be nothing *a priori* problematic in doing so.)

Once we fully integrate this message, we white Leftist men and women are free to leave behind the politically correct process of endless self-torturing guilt. Although Pascal Bruckner's critique of the contemporary Left often approaches the absurd,[22] this does not prevent him from occasionally generating pertinent insights—one cannot but agree with him when he detects in European politically correct self-flagellation an inverted form of clinging to one's superiority. Whenever the West is attacked, its first reaction is not aggressive defense but self-probing: what did we do to deserve it? We are ultimately to be blamed for the evils of the world; Third World catastrophes and terrorist violence are merely reactions to our crimes. The positive form of the White Man's Burden (his responsibility for civilizing the colonized barbarians) is thus merely replaced by its negative form (the burden of the white man's guilt): if we can no longer be the benevolent masters of the Third World, we can at least be the privileged source of evil, patronizingly depriving others of responsibility for their fate (when a Third World country engages in terrible crimes, it is never fully its own responsibility, but always an after-effect of colonization: they are merely imitating what their colonial masters used to do, and so on):

> We need our miserabilist clichés about Africa, Asia, Latin America, in order to confirm the cliché of a predatory, deadly West. Our noisy stigmatizations only serve to mask the wounded self-love: we no longer make the law. Other cultures know it, and they continue to culpabilize us only to escape our judgments on them.[23]

---

22 See, for example, his footnote elaborating on Alain Badiou's alleged anti-Semitism, in Bruckner's *La Tyrannie de la penitence*, Paris: Grasset 2006, p. 93.

23 Ibid., p. 49.

The West is thus caught in the typical superego predicament best rendered by Dostoyevsky's famous phrase from *The Brothers Karamazov*: "Each of us is guilty before everyone for everyone, and I more than the others." So the more the West confesses its crimes, the more it is made to feel culpable. This insight allows us also to detect a symmetric duplicity in the way certain Third World countries criticize the West: if the West's continuous self-excoriation functions as a desperate attempt to re-assert our superiority, the true reason why some in the Third World hate and reject the West lies not with the colonizing past and its continuing effects but with the self-critical spirit which the West has displayed in renouncing this past, with its implicit call to others to practise the same self-critical approach: "The West is not detested for its real faults, but for its attempt to amend them, because it was one of the first to try to tear itself out of its own bestiality, inviting the rest of the world to follow it."[24] The Western legacy is effectively not just that of (post)colonial imperialist domination, but also that of the self-critical examination of the violence and exploitation the West itself brought to the Third World. The French colonized Haiti, but the French Revolution also provided the ideological foundation for the rebellion which liberated the slaves and established an independent Haiti; the process of decolonization was set in motion when the colonized nations demanded for themselves the same rights that the West took for itself. In short, one should never forget that the West supplied the very standards by which it (and its critics) measures its own criminal past. We are dealing here with the dialectic of form and content: when colonial countries demand independence and enact a "return to roots," the very form of this return (that of an independent nation-state) is Western. In its very defeat (losing the colonies), the West thus wins, by imposing its social form on the other.

The lesson of Marx's two short 1853 articles on India ("The British Rule in India," "The Future Results of British Rule in India")—usually

---

24 Ibid., p. 51.

dismissed within postcolonial studies as embarrassing cases of Marx's "Eurocentrism"—are today more relevant than ever. Marx concedes without qualification the brutality and exploitative hypocrisy of the British colonization of India, up to and including the systematic use of torture prohibited in the West but "outsourced" to Indians (there really is nothing new under the sun—Guantanamos already existed in the midst of nineteenth-century British India): "The profound hypocrisy and inherent barbarism of bourgeois civilization lies unveiled before our eyes, turning from its home, where it assumes respectable forms, to the colonies, where it goes naked."[25] All Marx adds is that

> England has broken down the entire framework of Indian society, without any symptoms of reconstitution yet appearing. This loss of his old world, with no gain of a new one, imparts a particular kind of melancholy to the present misery of the Hindu, and separates Hindustan, ruled by Britain, from all its ancient traditions, and from the whole of its past history. . . . England, it is true, in causing a social revolution in Hindustan, was actuated only by the vilest interests, and was stupid in her manner of enforcing them. But that is not the question. The question is, can mankind fulfil its destiny without a fundamental revolution in the social state of Asia? If not, whatever may have been the crimes of England she was the unconscious tool of history in bringing about that revolution.[26]

One should not dismiss the talk of the "unconscious tool of history" as the expression of a naive teleology, of trust in the Cunning of Reason which makes even the vilest crimes instruments of progress—the point is simply that the British colonization of India created the conditions for the double liberation of India: from the constraints of its own tradition as well as from colonization itself. At a reception for Margaret Thatcher in 1985,

---

25 Karl Marx, "The Future Results of British Rule in India," in *Surveys From Exile*, edited and introduced by David Fernbach, Harmondsworth: Penguin 1973, p. 324

26 Karl Marx, "The British Rule in India," in ibid., pp. 302–3, 306–7.

the Chinese president applied to China Marx's statement about the role of British colonization in India: "The British occupation has awakened China from its age-old sleep."[27] Far from signaling continuous self-abasement in front of the ex-colonial powers, statements like these express true "post-postcolonialism," namely, a mature independence: to admit the positive effect of colonization, one has to be really free and be able to leave behind its stigma. (And, symmetrically, rejecting self-blame, while fully and—why not—proudly claiming one's emancipatory heritage, is a *sine qua non* for the renewal of the Left.)

Someone who cannot be accused of softness towards the colonizers is Frantz Fanon: his thoughts on the emancipatory power of violence are an embarrassment for many politically correct postcolonial theorists. However, as a perspicuous thinker trained in psychoanalysis, he also, back in 1952, provided the most poignant expression of the refusal to capitalize on the guilt of the colonizers:

I am a man, and what I have to recapture is the whole past of the world. I am not responsible solely for the slave revolt in Santo Domingo. Every time a man has contributed to the victory of the dignity of the spirit, every time a man has said no to an attempt to subjugate his fellows, I have felt solidarity with his act. In no way does my basic vocation have to be drawn from the past of peoples of color. In no way do I have to dedicate myself to reviving a black civilization unjustly ignored. I will not make myself the man of any past. . . . My black skin is not a repository for specific values. . . . Haven't I got better things to do on this earth than avenge the Blacks of the seventeenth century? . . . I as a man of color do not have the right to hope that in the white man there will be a crystallization of guilt toward the past of my race. I as a man of color do not have the right to seek ways of stamping down the pride of my former master. I have neither the right nor the duty to demand reparations for my subjugated ancestors. There is no black

---

27 Quoted from Bruckner, *La Tyrannie de la penitence*, p. 153.

mission; there is no white burden. . . . I do not want to be the victim of
the Ruse of a black world. . . . Am I going to ask today's white men to
answer for the slave traders of the seventeenth century? Am I going to
try by every means available to cause guilt to burgeon in their souls? . . .
I am not a slave to slavery that dehumanized my ancestors. . . . it would
be of enormous interest to discover a black literature or architecture
from the third century before Christ. We would be overjoyed to learn
of the existence of a correspondence between some black philosopher
and Plato. But we can absolutely not see how this fact would change the
lives of eight-year-old kids working in the cane fields of Martinique or
Guadeloupe. . . . I find myself in the world and I recognize that I have
one right alone: That of demanding human behavior from the other.[28]

Along the same lines, one should critically confront Sadri Khiari's
acerbic dismissal of French Leftists' attempts to provide proper papers
for the "*sans-papiers*" ("illegal" immigrants):

A White of the Left also has a weakness for the "*sans-papiers*." Undoubtedly
because the latter doesn't exist at all. And because, in order to exist just
a little bit, he is obliged to ask the Left for help. A *sans-papiers* doesn't
exist at all because, in order to exist, he has to threaten to finish off his
own existence. The proof that I exist, he says, is that I'm dying. And he
stops feeding himself. And the Left sees in this a good reason to denounce
the Right: "Give him the papers so that he will feed himself and cease to
exist!" Since, if he obtains the papers, he is no longer a *sans-papier*, and, if,
as a *sans-papier*, he didn't exist *at all*, when he has the papers, he just does
not exist, that's all. This is some progress.[29]

The underlying logic is clear and convincing: the "undocumented"
immigrant worker has no legal status, so that, if he is noticed at all, it is as

---

28   Frantz Fanon, *Black Skin, White Masks*, New York: Grove Press 2008, pp. 201–6.
29   Sadri Khiari, *La contre-révolution coloniale en France*, Paris: La fabrique 2009,
p. 11.

a dark external threat to our way of life; but once he gets his papers and his status is legalized, he again ceases to exist properly, since he becomes invisible in his specific situation. In a way, he becomes even more invisible once legalized: he is no longer a dark threat, but is fully normalized, drowned in the indistinct crowd of citizens. But what Khiari's dismissal nonetheless misses is how getting hold of "papers" opens up the space for further political self-organization and activity. Once one has the "papers," a vast field of political mobilization and pressure is opened up which, since it now involves legitimate citizens of "our" state, can no longer be dismissed as a dangerous menace from outside.

Furthermore, when we talk about anti-immigration measures, about the different forms of immigrant exclusion, and so on, we should always bear in mind that anti-immigration politics is *not* directly linked to capitalism or the interests of capital. The free circulation of labor is, on the contrary, in the interests of big capital, since cheaper immigrant labor will put pressure on "our own" workers to accept lower wages. And is outsourcing not also now an inverted form of employing immigrant workers? Resistance against immigrants is primarily the spontaneous-defensive reaction of the local working classes who (not wholly unjustifiably) perceive the immigrant worker as a new kind of strike-breaker and, as such, as an ally of capital. In short, it is global capital which is inherently multiculturalist and tolerant.

The standard position adopted by the unconditional defenders of the rights of illegal immigrants is to concede that, at the level of state, the counter-arguments may well be "true" (i.e., of course a country cannot accept an endless flow of immigrants; of course they compete in ways which threaten local jobs, and may also pose certain security risks), but their defense moves at a different level altogether, a level which has a direct link with demands of reality, the level of principled politics where we can unconditionally insist that "*qui est ici est d'ici*" ("those who are here are from here"). But is this principled position not all too simple, allowing for the comfortable position of a beautiful soul? I insist on my principles, and let the state deal with pragmatic constraints of reality . . . In this way, do we not avoid a crucial aspect of the political battle for the rights of immigrants: how to convince the workers opposing those immigrants that they are fighting the wrong battle; and how to propose a feasible form of alternative politics? The "impossible" (an openness to immigrants) has to happen in reality—*this* would be a true political event.

But why should the immigrant not be satisfied with his normalization? Because, instead of asserting his identity, he has to adapt to his oppressor's standards: he is accepted, but *de facto* in a secondary role. His oppressor's discourse defines the terms of his identity. One should remember here the programmatic words of Stokely Carmichael (the founder of Black Power): "We have to fight for the right to invent the terms which will allow us to define ourselves and to define our relations to society, and we have to fight that these terms will be accepted. This is the first need of a free people, and this is also the first right refused by every oppressor." The problem is how, exactly, to do this. That is to say, how to resist the temptation to define oneself with reference to some mythical and totally external identity ("African roots"), which, by way of cutting links with "white" culture, also deprives the oppressed of crucial intellectual tools for their struggle (namely, the egalitarian-emancipatory tradition) as well as potential allies. One should thus slightly correct Carmichael's words: what the oppressors really fear is not some totally mythical self-definition with no links to white culture, but a self-definition which, by way of appropriating key elements of the "white" egalitarian-emancipatory tradition, *redefines that very tradition*, transforming it not so much in terms of what it says as in what it *does not* say—that is, obliterating the implicit qualifications which have *de facto* excluded Blacks from the egalitarian space. In other words, it is not enough to find new terms with which to define oneself outside of the dominant white tradition—one should go a step further and deprive the whites of the monopoly on defining *their own* tradition.

In this precise sense, the Haitian Revolution was "a defining moment in world history."[30] The point is not to study the Haitian Revolution as

---

30 Buck-Morss, *Hegel, Haiti, and Universal History*, p. 13.

an extension of the European revolutionary spirit, that is, to examine the significance of Europe (of the French Revolution) for the Haitian Revolution, but rather to assert *the significance of the Haitian Revolution for Europe*. It is not only that one cannot understand Haiti without Europe—one cannot understand either the scope or the limitations of the European emancipation process without Haiti. Haiti was an exception from the very beginning, from its revolutionary struggle against slavery which ended in independence in January 1804: "Only in Haiti was the declaration of human freedom universally consistent. Only in Haiti was this declaration sustained at all costs, in direct opposition to the social order and economic logic of the day." For this reason, "there is no single event in the whole of modern history whose implications were more threatening to the dominant global order of things."[31]

One of the organizers of the rebellion was a black slave preacher known as "John Bookman," a name designating him as literate; surprisingly, the "book" his name refers to was not the Bible but the Qur'an. This brings to mind the great tradition of millenarian "communist" rebellions in Islam, especially the "Qarmatian republic" and the Zanj revolt.[32] The Qarmatians were a millenarian Ismaili group centered in eastern Arabia (today's Bahrain), where they established a utopian republic in 899. They are often denounced for instigating a "century of terrorism": during the 930 Hajj season, they seized the Black Stone from Mecca—an act taken to signal that the age of love had arrived, such that one no longer had to obey the Law. The Qarmatians' goal was to build a society based on reason and equality. The state was governed by a council of six with a chief who was a first among equals. All property within the community was distributed evenly among all initiates. Although the Qarmatians were organized as an esoteric society, they were not a secret one: their activities were public and openly propagated.

What is even more crucial is that their rise was instigated by the slave

---

31   Peter Hallward, *Damming the Flood*, New York: Verso 2008.
32   The following account relies heavily upon the relevant Wikipedia entries; see in particular the entries on the "Qarmatians" and the "Zanj Rebellion."

rebellion in Basra which disrupted the power of Baghdad. This "Zanj Revolt," which took place over a period of fifteen years (869–83), involved over 500,000 slaves who had been imported to the region from across the Muslim empire. Their leader, Ali ibn Muhammad, was shocked by the suffering of the slaves working in the Basra marshes; he began to inquire into their working conditions and nutritional standards. He claimed to be a descendent of Caliph Ali ibn Abu Talib; when his claim to this lineage was not accepted, he started to preach the radically egalitarian doctrine of the Kharijites, according to which the most qualified man should reign, even if he was an Abyssinian slave. No wonder, again, that the official historians (such as Al-Tabari and Al-Masudi) noted only the "vicious and brutal" character of the uprising . . .

But there is no need to go more than a thousand years back to find this dimension of Islam—a glance at the events that followed the 2009 presidential election in Iran is sufficient. The green color adopted by Mousavi supporters, the cries of "Allah akbar!" that resonated from the roofs of Tehran in the evening darkness, clearly indicate that they saw their mobilization as a repetition of the 1979 Khomeini revolution, as the return to its roots, undoing the revolution's later corruption. This return to the origins is not only programmatic; it even more concerns the mode of activity of the crowds: the emphatic unity of the people, their all-encompassing solidarity, creative self-organization, improvising manners to articulate protest, the unique mixture of spontaneity and discipline, like the ominous march of thousands in complete silence. This was a genuine popular uprising of the disappointed partisans of the Khomeini revolution. This is why one should compare the events in Iran to the US intervention in Iraq: Iran provided a case of genuine assertion of popular will as against the foreign imposition of democracy in Iraq. And this is also why the events in Iran may be read as a comment on the platitudes of Obama's Cairo speech which focused on the dialogue between religions: we do not need the dialogue between religions (between civilizations), we need a link of solidarity between those who struggle for justice in Muslim countries and those who participate in the same struggle elsewhere. In other words, we require a politicization process which strengthens the struggle here, there and everywhere.

There are a couple of crucial consequences to be drawn from this insight. First, Ahmadinejad is not the hero of the Islamist poor, but a genuine corrupted Islamo-Fascist populist, a kind of Iranian Berlusconi whose mixture of clownish posturing and ruthless power-politics causes unease even among the majority of ayatollahs. His demagogic distribution of crumbs to the poor should not deceive us: behind him are not only organs of police repression and a very Westernized PR apparatus, but also a strong new class of the rich, the result of the regime's corruption (Iran's Revolutionary Guards are not a working class militia, but a mega-corporation, the strongest center of wealth in the country). Second, one should draw a clear difference between the two main candidates opposed to Ahmadinejad, Mehdi Karroubi and Mousavi. Karroubi effectively is a reformist, basically proposing the Iranian version of clientalism, promising favors to all the particular groups. Mousavi is something entirely different: his name stands for a genuine resuscitation of the popular dreams which sustained the Khomeini revolution. Even if this dream was a utopia, one should recognize in it the genuine utopia of the revolution itself. For the 1979 Khomeini revolution cannot be reduced to a hard line Islamist takeover—it was so much more. Now is the time to remember the incredible effervescence of the first year after the revolution, with the breathtaking explosion of political and social creativity, organizational experiments and debates among students and ordinary people. The very fact that this explosion had to be stifled demonstrates that the Khomeini revolution was an authentic political event, a momentary *opening* that unleashed previously unimaginable forces of social transformation, a moment in which "everything seemed possible." What followed was a gradual closing down through the take-over of political power by the theocratic establishment. To put it in Freudian terms, the recent protest movement is the "return of repressed" of the Khomeini revolution. Whatever the outcome in Iran, it is vitally important to keep in mind that we witnessed a great emancipatory event which does not fit into the frame of a struggle between pro-Western liberals and anti-Western fundamentalists. If our cynical pragmatism makes us lose the capacity to recognize this emancipatory dimension, then we in the West are effectively entering a post-democratic era, getting ready for our own Ahmadinejads. Italians already know his name: Berlusconi. Others are waiting in line.

What was it, then, about the Haitian Revolution that went beyond Kantian enthusiasm, and that Hegel clearly saw? What needs to be added here, moving beyond Kant, is that there are social groups which, on account of their lacking a determinate place in the "private" order of the social hierarchy—in other words, as a "part of no-part" of the social body—directly stand for universality. Properly communist revolutionary enthusiasm is unconditionally rooted in full solidarity with this "part of no-part" and its position of singular universality. The Haitian Revolution "failed" when it betrayed this solidarity and developed into a new hierarchical-nationalist community in which the new local black elite continued the exploitation process. The reason for its failure was not the "backwardness" of Haiti. It failed because it was *ahead* of its time—its slave plantations (mostly sugarcane) were not a remainder of premodern societies, but models of efficient capitalist production; the discipline to which slaves were submitted served as an example for the discipline to which wage-laborers were later submitted in capitalist metropolises. After the abolition of slavery, the new black Haiti government imposed "agrarian militarism"—in order not to disturb the production of sugarcane for export, ex-slaves were obliged to continue working at their plantations under the same owners, only now as technically "free" wage-laborers. The tension that characterizes a bourgeois society—democratic enthusiasm and personal freedoms co-existing with slave-like work discipline—this slavery *in* equality appeared in Haiti in its most radical form. What makes capital exceptional is its unique combination of the values of freedom and equality and the facts of exploitation and domination: the gist of Marx's analysis is that the legal-ideological matrix of freedom-equality is not a mere "mask" concealing exploitation-domination, but the very *form* in which the latter is exercised.

The Capitalist Exception

There is a recurring problem which we encounter again here: the fate of the Haitian Revolution, its regression into a new form of hierarchical rule (after the death of Dessalines), is one in a series of reversals that characterize modern revolutions—the passage from the Jacobins to Napoleon, from the October Revolution to Stalin, from Mao's Cultural Revolution to Deng Xiaoping's capitalism. How are we to read this passage? Is the second phase (the Thermidor) the "truth" of the first revolutionary phase (as Marx sometimes seems to claim), or is it just that in each case the revolutionary evental series exhausted itself?

I claim here that the communist Idea persists: it survives the failures of its realization as a specter which returns again and again, in an endless persistence best captured in the already-quoted words from Beckett's *Worstward Ho*: "Try again. Fail again. Fail better." This brings us to the crux of the matter. One of the mantras of the postmodern Left has been that we should finally leave behind the "Jacobin–Leninist" paradigm of centralized dictatorial power. But perhaps the time has now come to turn this mantra around and admit that a good dose of just that "Jacobin–Leninist" paradigm is precisely what the Left needs today. Now, more than ever, one should insist on what Badiou calls the "eternal" Idea of Communism, or the communist "invariants"—the "four fundamental concepts" at work from Plato through the medieval millenarian revolts and on to Jacobinism, Leninism and Maoism: strict *egalitarian justice*, disciplinary *terror*, political *voluntarism*, and *trust in the people*. This matrix is not "superseded" by any new postmodern or postindustrial or post-whatever-you-want dynamic. However, up until the present historical moment, this eternal Idea functioned as, precisely, a Platonic Idea which persisted, returning again and again after every defeat. What is missing today is—to put it in philosophico-theological terms—a privileged link of the Idea to a singular historical moment (in the same way that, in Christianity, the whole eternal divine edifice stands and falls with the contingent event of the birth and death of Christ).

There is something unique in today's constellation: many perspicuous analysts have noted that contemporary capitalism poses a problem to this logic of a resistance which persists. Brian Massumi, for example, has formulated clearly how contemporary capitalism overcame the logic of totalizing normality and adopted the logic of erratic excess.[33] And one can supplement this analysis in many directions—the very process of subtracting oneself and creating "liberated territories" outside the domain of state has been reappropriated by capital. Exemplary of the logic of global capitalism are the so-called "Special Economic Zones": geographical regions within a (usually Third World) state with economic laws which are more liberal than the state's standard economic laws (allowing for, e.g., lower import and export taxes, the free flow of capital, the limitation or direct prohibition of trade unions, no minimum working day, and so on) in order to increase foreign investments. The name itself covers a whole range of more specific zone types: Free Trade Zones, Export Processing Zones, Free Zones, Industrial Estates, Free Ports, Urban Enterprise Zones, etc. With their unique combination of "openness" (as a free space partially exempt from state sovereignty) and closure (enforcement of working conditions unencumbered by legally guaranteed freedoms), which renders possible heightened levels of exploitation, these zones are the structural counterparts to our celebrated communities of "intellectual labor"—they constitute a fourth term to be added to the tetrad of high-tech "intellectual labor," gated communities, and slums.

---

33   See my *In Defense of Lost Causes*, London: Verso 2008, p. 197

Badiou also recognizes the exceptional *ontological* status of capitalism, whose dynamic undermines every stable frame of re-presentation: the task usually performed by critico-political activity (that of undermining the re-presentational frame of the state) is already performed by capitalism itself—which poses a problem for Badiou's notion of "evental" politics. In pre-capitalist formations, every state, every re-presentational totalization, implied a founding exclusion, a point of "symptomal torsion," a "part of no-part," an element which, although part of the system, had no proper place within it—emancipatory politics then had to intervene from the position of this excessive ("supernumerary") element which, although part of the situation, could not be *accounted for* in its terms. But what happens when the system no longer excludes the excess, and instead directly posits it as its driving force—as is the case in capitalism, which can only reproduce itself through its constant self-revolutionizing, through the constant overcoming of its own limits? To put it another way: if a political event, an emancipatory intervention into a determinate historical world, is always linked to the excessive point of its "symptomal torsion"—if, by definition, it undermines the contours of that world—how then are we to make a political intervention into a universe which is in itself already world-less, which, for its reproduction, no longer needs to be contained by the constraints of a "world"? As Alberto Toscano notes in his perspicuous analysis, Badiou gets caught up here in an inconsistency when he draws the "logical" conclusion that, in a "world-less" universe (which is today's universe of global capitalism), the aim of emancipatory politics should be the precise opposite of its "traditional" *modus operandi*—the task today is to form a new world, to propose new Master-Signifiers that would provide "cognitive mapping."[34]

The contours of the dilemma should thus be clear. Our starting point was the logic of resistance/subtraction: communism is an eternal

---

34 Alberto Toscano, "From the state to the world? Badiou and anti-capitalism," *Communication & Cognition*, Vol. 36 (2003), pp. 1–2.

Idea which persists, exploding from time to time... But what if, for example, the Chinese Cultural Revolution represented not only the exhaustion of the state-party epoch, but the end of that very process in which egalitarian-emancipatory projects explode and then reverse into the "normal" run of things? Here the series is terminated, simply because the enemy has now taken over the revolutionizing dynamic: one can no longer play the game of subverting the Order from the position of its "part of no-part," since the Order already now entails its own permanent subversion. With the full deployment of capitalism, it is "normal" life itself which, in a certain manner, is "carnivalized," with its constant reversals, crises, and reinventions, and it is the critique of capitalism, from a "stable" ethical position, which today more than ever appears as an exception.

The true question here is: how is externality with regard to the state to be operationalized? Since the Cultural Revolution signals the failure of the attempt to destroy the state from within, to abolish the state, is the alternative then simply to accept the state as a fact, as the apparatus which takes care of "servicing the goods," and to operate at a distance towards it (bombarding it with prescriptive proclamations and demands)? Or is it, more radically, that we should aim at a subtraction *from* the hegemonic field which, simultaneously, violently intervenes *into* this field, reducing it to its occluded minimal difference? Such a subtraction is extremely violent, even more violent than destruction/purification: it is reduction to the minimal difference of part(s)/no-part, 1 and 0, groups and the proletariat. It is not only a subtraction of the subject *from* the hegemonic field, but a subtraction which violently *affects* this field itself, laying bare its true coordinates. Such a subtraction does not add a third position to the two positions whose tension characterizes the hegemonic field (so that we now have, along with liberalism and fundamentalism, a radical Leftist emancipatory politics). The third term rather "denaturalizes" the whole hegemonic field, bringing out the underlying complicity of the opposed poles that constitute it. Therein resides the dilemma of subtraction: is it a subtraction/

withdrawal which leaves the field from which it withdraws intact (or which even functions as its inherent supplement, like the "subtraction" or withdrawal from social reality into one's true Self proposed by New Age meditation); or does it violently perturb the field from which it withdraws? "Subtraction" is thus what Kant called an amphibious concept. Paraphrasing Lenin, one can say that everything, up to and including the fate of radical emancipatory movements today, hinges on how we read this concept, on what word which will be attached to it or dissociated from it.

Badiou's "subtraction," like Hegel's *Aufhebung*, contains three different layers of meaning: (1) to withdraw, disconnect; (2) to reduce the complexity of a situation to its minimal difference; (3) to destroy the existing order. As in Hegel, the solution is not to differentiate the three meanings (eventually proposing a specific term for each of them), but to grasp subtraction as the unity of its three dimensions: one should withdraw from being immersed in a situation in such a way that the withdrawal renders visible the "minimal difference" sustaining the situation's multiplicity, and thereby causes its disintegration, just as the withdrawal of a single card from a house of cards causes the collapse of the entire edifice.

Of course, egalitarian-emancipatory "de-territorialization" is not the same as the postmodern-capitalist form, but it nonetheless radically changes the terms of the emancipatory struggle. In particular, the enemy is no longer the established hierarchical order of a state. How, then, are we to revolutionize an order whose very principle is constant self-revolutionizing? More than a solution to the problems we are facing today, communism is itself the name of a problem: a name for the difficult task of breaking out of the confines of the market-and-state framework, a task for which no quick formula is at hand. "It's just the simple thing that's hard, so hard to do," as Brecht put it in his "In Praise of Communism."

The Hegelian answer is that the problem or deadlock is its own solution—but not in the simple or direct sense that capitalism is already in itself communism, and that only a purely formal reversal is needed. My suggestion is rather this: what if today's global capitalism, precisely insofar as it is "world-less," involving a constant disruption of all fixed order, opens up the space for a revolution which will break the vicious cycle of revolt and its reinscription, which will, in other words, no longer follow the pattern of an evental explosion followed by a return to normality, but will instead assume the task of a *new "ordering" against the global capitalist disorder*? Out of revolt we should shamelessly pass to enforcing a new order. (Is this not one of the lessons of the ongoing financial meltdown?) This is why the focus on capitalism is crucial if we want to reactualize the communist Idea: contemporary "world-less" capitalism radically changes the very coordinates of the communist struggle—the enemy is no longer the state to be undermined from its point of symptomal torsion, but a flux of permanent self-revolutionizing.

Consequently, I want to propose two axioms concerning the relationship between the state and politics: (1) The failure of communist state–party politics is above all and primarily the failure of anti-statal politics, of the endeavor to break out of the constraints of the state, to replace statal forms of organization with "direct" non-representative forms of self-organization ("councils"). (2) If you have no clear idea of what you want to replace the state with, you have no right to subtract/withdraw from the state. Instead of taking a distance from the state, the true task should be to make the state itself work in a non-statal mode. The alternative "either struggle for state power (which makes us the same as the enemy we are fighting) or resist by withdrawing to a position of distance from the state" is false—both its terms share the same premise, that the state-form, in the way we know it today, is here to stay, so that all we can do is either take over the state or take a distance towards it. Here, one should shamelessly repeat the lesson of Lenin's *State and Revolution*: the goal of revolutionary violence is not to take over state power, but to transform it, radically changing its functioning, its relationship to its base, and so on.[35] Therein resides the key component of the "dictatorship of the proletariat."

The only appropriate conclusion to be drawn from this insight is that the "dictatorship of the proletariat" is a kind of (necessary) oxymoron, *not* a state-form in which proletariat is now the ruling class. We are dealing with the "dictatorship of the proletariat" only when the state itself is radically transformed, relying on new forms of popular participation. This is why there was more than mere hypocrisy in the fact that, at the highest point of Stalinism, when the entire social edifice had been shattered by the purges, the new constitution proclaimed the end of the "class" character of Soviet power (voting rights were restored to members of classes previously excluded), and the socialist regimes were called "people's democracies"—a sure indication indeed that they were not "dictatorships of the proletariat." But, again, how are we to achieve such a "dictatorship"?

Capitalism with Asian Values . . . in Europe

Peter Sloterdijk (definitely not one of our side, but also not a complete idiot) remarked that if there is one person to whom they will build monuments a hundred years from now, it is Lee Quan Yew, the Singaporean leader who invented and realized so-called "capitalism with Asian values." The virus of this authoritarian form of capitalism is slowly but surely spreading around the globe. Before setting in motion his reforms, Deng Xiaoping visited Singapore and expressly praised it as a model for all of China to follow. This development has a

---

35 Badiou himself was on the right track when, years ago, he wrote in *Ethics* (New York: Verso 2002): "The realization of the world as global market, the undivided reign of great financial conglomerates, etc., all this is an indisputable reality and one that conforms, essentially, to Marx's analysis. The question is, where does politics fit in with all this? What kind of politics is really heterogeneous to what capital demands?—that is today's question." The implication of these lines is that, today, authentic emancipatory politics has to define itself through its active opposition to the universe of the capital—it has to be "anti-capitalist."

world-historical meaning: until now, capitalism seemed inextricably linked with democracy— from time to time there were, of course, relapses into direct dictatorship, but, after a decade or two, democracy once again imposed itself (recall the cases of South Korea and Chile). Now, however, the link between democracy and capitalism has been definitely broken.

Faced with the contemporary explosion of capitalism in China, analysts often ask when political democracy as the "natural" political accompaniment of capitalism will assert itself. A closer analysis, however, quickly dispels this hope—what if the promised democratic second stage that follows the authoritarian valley of tears never arrives? This, perhaps, is what is so unsettling about China today: the suspicion that its version of authoritarian capitalism is not merely a remainder of our past—a repetition of the process of capitalist accumulation which, in Europe, went on from the sixteenth to the eighteenth century—but a sign of the future. What if the "vicious combination of the Asian *knout* and the European stock market" (Trotsky's characterization of tsarist Russia) proves itself to be economically more efficient than liberal capitalism? What if it signals that democracy, as we understand it, is no longer a condition and motive force of economic development, but rather an obstacle?

Some naive Leftists claim that it is the legacy of the Cultural Revolution and Maoism in general which acts as a counter-force to unbridled capitalism, preventing its worst excesses, maintaining a minimum of social solidarity. What if, however, exactly the opposite is the case? What if, in a kind of unintended and for this reason all the more cruelly ironic Cunning of Reason, the Cultural Revolution, with its brutal erasure of past traditions, was a "shock" which created the conditions for the ensuing capitalist explosion? What if China has to be added to Naomi Klein's list of states in which a natural, military or social catastrophe cleared the way for a new capitalist explosion?[36]

---

36   In her *Shock Doctrine*, Klein has a chapter on China in which she locates the

The supreme irony of history is thus that it was Mao himself who created the ideological conditions for the rapid development of capitalism in China by tearing apart the fabric of traditional society. What was his call to the people, especially the young, in the Cultural Revolution? Don't wait for someone else to tell you what to do, you have the right to rebel! So think and act for yourselves, destroy cultural relics, denounce and attack not only your elders, but also government and party officials! Sweep away the repressive state mechanisms and organize yourself in communes! And Mao's call was heard—what followed was an explosion of unrestrained passion for de-legitimizing all forms of authority, such that, at the end, Mao had to call in the army to restore some order. The paradox is thus that the key battle of the Cultural Revolution was not between the Communist Party apparatus and its traditionalist enemies, but between the army and the Party, on the one hand, and the forces Mao himself had called into being on the other.[37]

What this means, of course, is not that we should renounce democracy on behalf of capitalist progress, but that we should confront the limitations of parliamentary democracy, nicely formulated by Noam Chomsky when he noted that "it is only when the threat of popular participation is overcome that democratic forms can be safely contemplated."[38] He thereby identified the "passivizing" core of

---

shock that set in motion the capitalist development in the Tiananmen demonstrations and their violent suppression, not in the Cultural Revolution. The nice irony of this link is that capitalism was offered to the Chinese people as a reply to their demands: "You want democracy? Here you have its real foundation!" However, it is doubtful if the Tiananmen events were really a profound shock for the whole of China.

37   Asked about his next project, Jia Zhangke, the film director who, up until then had focused on the subjective impact of China's explosive capitalist development, answered: "A fiction set in the 1970–75 period. Two groups of young people struggle for control of a city during the cultural revolution. . . . I really do think that the answer to the question asked today in China, that entire relation to development, is deeply rooted in the cultural revolution, in what happened at that time." (From the booklet accompanying the BFI DVD-edition of *Still Life*, p. 16.) Jia Zhangke here provides here a refined insight into the link between the Cultural Revolution and the ongoing capitalist revolution.

38   Noam Chomsky, *Necessary Illusions*, Cambridge: South End Press 1999, p. 69.

parliamentary democracy which makes it incompatible with the direct political self-organization of the people.

Walter Lippmann, the icon of American journalism in the twentieth century, played a key role in the self-understanding of US democracy. Although politically progressive (advocating a fair policy towards the Soviet Union, etc.), he proposed a theory of the public media which has a chilling truth effect. He coined the term "Manufacturing Consent," later made famous by Chomsky, although Lippmann intended it in a positive way. In *Public Opinion* (1922), he wrote that a "governing class" must rise to face the challenge—he saw the public as Plato did, as a great beast or a bewildered herd, floundering in the "chaos of local opinions."[39] So the herd of citizens must be governed by "a specialized class whose interests reach beyond the locality"—this elite class is to act as a machinery of knowledge that circumvents the primary defect of democracy, the impossible ideal of the "omni-competent citizen." This is indeed how our democracies function—and with our consent. There is no mystery in what Lippmann was saying, it is an obvious fact; the mystery is that, knowing this, we continue to play the game. We act *as if* we are free to choose, while silently not only accepting but even *demanding* that an invisible injunction (inscribed in the very form of our commitment to "free speech") tells us what to do and to think. As Marx noted long ago, the secret is in the form itself.

In this sense, in a democracy, every ordinary citizen is effectively a king—but a king in a constitutional democracy, a monarch who decides only formally, whose function is merely to sign off on measures proposed by an executive administration. This is why the problem with democratic rituals is homologous to the great problem of constitutional monarchy: how to protect the dignity of the king? How to maintain the appearance that the king effectively makes decisions, when we all know this not to be true? Trotsky was thus right in his basic reproach to parliamentary democracy, which was not that it gives

---

39   Walter Lippman, *Public Opinionn*, Charleston: BiblioLife 2008.

too much power to the uneducated masses, but, paradoxically, that *it passivizes the masses, leaving the initiative with the apparatus of state power (in contrast to the "soviets" in which the working classes directly mobilize themselves and exert power)*.[40] What we refer to as the "crisis of democracy" occurs not, therefore, when people stop believing in their own power, but, on the contrary, when they stop trusting the elites, those who are supposed to know for them and provide the guidelines, when they experience the anxiety accompanying the recognition that "the (true) throne is empty," that the decision is now *really* theirs. This is why in "free elections" there is always a minimal aspect of politeness: those in power politely pretend that they do not really hold power, and ask us to decide freely if we want to give them power—in a way which mirrors the logic of a gesture meant to be refused.

To put it in the terms of the Will: representative democracy in its very notion involves a passivization of the popular Will, its transformation into non-willing—willing is transferred onto an agent which re-presents the people and wills on its account. Whenever one is accused of undermining democracy, one's answer should thus be a paraphrase of the reply given by Marx and Engels to a similar reproach (that communism undermines the family, property, freedom, etc.) in *The Communist Manifesto*: the ruling order is itself already doing all the undermining necessary. In the same way that (market) freedom is unfreedom for those who sell their labor-power, in the same way that the family is undermined by the bourgeois family as legalized prostitution, democracy is undermined by the parliamentary form with its concomitant passivization of the large majority, as well as by the growing executive power implied by the increasingly influential logic of the emergency state.

Badiou has proposed a distinction between two types (or, rather, levels) of corruption in democracy: *de facto* empirical corruption, and the corruption that pertains to the very form of democracy with

---

40 See Leon Trotsky, *Terrorism and Communism*, London: Verso Books 2007.

its reduction of politics to the negotiation of private interests. This gap becomes visible in those rare cases of an honest "democratic" politician who, while fighting empirical corruption, nonetheless sustains the formal space of corruption. (There is, of course, also the opposite case of the empirically corrupt politician who acts on behalf of the dictatorship of virtue.) In terms of the Benjaminian distinction between constituted and constituent violence, one could say that we are dealing with a difference between "constituted" corruption (empirical cases of law breaking) and the "constituent" corruption of the democratic form of government itself:

> For if democracy means representation, it is first of all the representation of the general system that bears its forms. In other words: electoral democracy is only representative in so far as it is first of all the consensual representation of capitalism, or of what today has been renamed the "market economy." This is its underlying corruption…[41]

One should take these lines in the strictest transcendental sense: at the empirical level, of course, multi-party liberal democracy "represents"—mirrors, registers, measures—the quantitative dispersal of different opinions, what people think about the proposed programs of the parties and about their candidates, and so on; however, prior to this empirical level, and in a much more radical "transcendental" sense, multi-party liberal democracy *"represents"— instantiates—a certain vision of society, politics, and the role of the individuals within it*. Liberal democracy "represents" a very precise vision of social life in which politics is organized by parties which compete through elections to exert control over the state legislative and executive apparatus, and so on and so forth. One should always be aware that this "transcendental frame" is never neutral—it privileges certain values and practises. This

---

41   Badiou, *The Meaning of Sarkozy*, p. 91.

non-neutrality becomes palpable in moments of crisis or indifference, when we experience the inability of the democratic system to register what people really want or think—an inability signaled by anomalous phenomena such as the UK elections of 2005 when, in spite of the growing unpopularity of Tony Blair (who was regularly voted the most unpopular person in the UK), there was no way for this discontent to find a politically effective expression. Something was obviously very wrong here—it was not that people "did not know what they wanted," but rather that cynical resignation prevented them from acting upon it, so that the result was a weird gap between what people thought and how they acted (voted).

Plato, in his critique of democracy, was fully aware of this second form of corruption, and his critique is also clearly discernible in the Jacobin privileging of Virtue: in democracy, in the sense of the representation of and negotiation between a plurality of private interests, there is no place for Virtue. This is why, in a proletarian revolution, democracy has to be replaced by the *dictatorship* of the proletariat.

There is no reason to despise democratic elections; the point is only to insist that they are not *per se* an indication of Truth—on the contrary, as a rule, they tend to reflect the predominant *doxa* determined by the hegemonic ideology. Let us take an example which is surely not problematic: France in 1940. Even Jacques Duclos, second in charge of the French Communist Party, admitted in a private conversation that if at that point free elections had been held in France, Marshal Pétain would have won with 90 percent of the votes. When de Gaulle, in his historic act, refused capitulation to Germany and claimed that only he, not the Vichy regime, spoke on behalf of the true France (not only on behalf of the "majority of the French"!), what he was saying was deeply true even if "democratically" speaking it was not only without legitimization, but was clearly opposed to the opinion of the majority of French people. There *can* be democratic elections which enact an event of Truth—elections in which, against sceptical-cynical inertia, the majority momentarily "awakens" and votes against the hegemony of ideological opinion. However, the very exceptional nature of such an occurrence proves that elections as such are not a medium of Truth.

It is this, the authentic potential of democracy, which is now losing ground to the rise of authoritarian capitalism, whose tentacles are inching closer and closer to the West. In each country, of course, in accordance with its own "values": Putin's capitalism with "Russian values" (the brutal display of power), Berlusconi's capitalism with "Italian values" (comical posturing). Both Putin and Berlusconi rule in democracies which are increasingly being reduced to empty ritualized shells, and in spite of the rapidly worsening economic situation they both enjoy a high level of popular support (over 60 percent in the polls). No wonder they are personal friends: both have a tendency towards occasional "spontaneous" scandalous outbursts (which, at least in the case of Putin, are well-prepared in advance so that they fit the Russian "national character"). From time to time, Putin likes to use a common dirty word or make an obscene threat—when, a couple of years ago, a Western journalist asked him an unpleasant question about Chechnya, Putin snapped back that if the journalist had not yet been circumcised he was cordially invited to Moscow, where they have excellent surgeons who would do the work with gusto. . .

From Profit to Rent

Whence this resurgence of direct, non-democratic authority? Above and beyond any cultural factors involved, there is an inner necessity for this resurgence in the very logic of contemporary capitalism. That is to say, the central problem we are facing today is how the predominance (or even hegemonic role) of "intellectual labor" within late capitalism affects Marx's basic scheme of the separation of labor from its objective conditions, and of the revolution as the subjective re-appropriation of those conditions. In spheres like the World Wide Web, production, exchange and consumption are inextricably intertwined, potentially even identified: my product is immediately communicated to and consumed by another. Marx's classic notion of commodity fetishism in which "relations between people" assume the form of "relations between things" has thus to be radically re-thought: in "immaterial labor," "relations between people" are "not so much hidden beneath the veneer of objectivity, but are themselves the very material of our everyday exploitation,"[42] so we cannot any longer talk about "reification" in the classic Lukácsian sense. Far from being invisible, social relationality in its very fluidity is directly the object of marketing and exchange: in "cultural capitalism," one no longer sells (and buys) objects which "bring" cultural or emotional experiences, one directly sells (and buys) such experiences.

While one has to admit that Negri does here have a grip on the key question, his answer seems inadequate. His starting point is Marx's thesis in the *Grundrisse* on the radical transformation of the status of the "fixed capital":

The development of fixed capital indicates to what degree general social knowledge has become a direct force of production, and to what degree, hence, the conditions of the process of social life itself have come under the control of the general intellect and been transformed in accordance with it. To what degree the powers of social production have been produced, not only in the form of knowledge, but also as immediate organs of social practice, of the real life process.[43]

With the development of general social knowledge, the "productive power of labour" is thus "itself the greatest productive power. From the standpoint of the direct production process it can be regarded as the production of fixed capital, this fixed capital being man himself."[44] And, again, since capital organizes its exploitation by appearing as "fixed capital"

---

42 Nina Power, "Dissing," *Radical Philosophy* 154, p. 55.
43 Karl Marx, *Grundrisse*, translated with a foreword by Martin Nicolaus, Harmondsworth: Penguin 1973, p. 706.
44 Ibid.

against living labor, the moment the key component of fixed capital is "man himself," "general social knowledge," the very social foundation of capitalist exploitation is undermined, and the role of capital becomes purely parasitic. According to the Negrian perspective, with today's global interactive media, creative inventiveness is no longer individual, it is immediately collectivized, part of the "commons," so that any attempt to privatize it through copy-righting becomes problematic—more and more literally, "property is theft" here. So what about a company like Microsoft which does precisely this—organizing and exploiting the collective synergy of creative cognitive singularities? The only remaining task seems to be to imagine how cognitive workers will "eliminate bosses, because industrial control over cognitive work is completely *dépassé*."[45] What new social movements signal is that "the wage epoch is over, and that we have passed from the confrontation between work and capital concerning wages to the confrontation between the multitude and the State concerning the instauration of the citizen's income."[46] Therein resides the basic feature of "today's social revolutionary transition": "One has to bring capital to recognize the weight and importance of the common good, and if capital is not ready to do it, one has to compel it."[47] Note Negri's precise formulation: not "abolish" capital, but "compel it" to recognize the common good, in other words, one remains within capitalism—if there ever was a utopian idea, this is surely one. Here is how Negri describes the proximity of contemporary biopolitical capitalism to the direct assertion of the productivity of the multitude:

> The picture is one of a circulation of commodities, webs of information, continuous movements, and radical nomadism of labour, and the ferocious exploitation of these dynamics ... but also of constant and inexhaustible *excess*, of the biopolitical power of the multitude and of

---

45   Toni Negri, *Goodbye Mr. Socialism*, Rome: Feltrinelli 2006, p. 234
46   Ibid., p. 204.
47   Ibid., p. 235.

its excess with regard to the structural controlling ability of dominant institutions. All of the available energies are put to work, society is put to work ... Within this exploited totality and injunction to work lies an intransitive freedom that is irreducible to the control that tries to subdue it. Even though freedom can run against itself, ... lines of flight still open up in this ambivalence: suffering is often productive but never revolutionary; what is revolutionary is excess, overflow, and power.[48]

What we find here is the standard post-Hegelian matrix of the productive flux which is always in excess with regard to the structural totality which tries to subdue and control it ... But what if, in a parallax shift, we perceive *the capitalist network itself as the true excess over the flow of the productive multitude*? What if, while the contemporary production of the multitude directly produces life, it continues to produce an excess (which is even functionally superfluous), the excess of Capital? Why do immediately produced relations still need the mediating role of capitalist relations? What if the true enigma is why continuous nomadic "molecular" movement needs a parasitic "molar" structure which (deceptively) appears as an obstacle to its unleashed productivity? Why, the moment we abolish this obstacle/excess, do we lose the productive flux constrained by the parasitic excess? And this also means that we should invert the topic of fetishism, of "relations between people appearing as relations between things": what if the direct "production of life" celebrated by Hardt and Negri is falsely transparent? What if, in it, the invisible "relations between [immaterial] things [of Capital] appear as direct relations between people"?

Here, more than ever, it is crucial to remember the lesson of the Marxist dialectic of fetishization: the "reification" of relations between people (the fact that they assume the form of phantasmagorical "relations between things") is always redoubled by the apparently opposite process, by the false "personalization" ("psychologization")

---

48   Toni Negri, "On Rem Koolhaas," *Radical Philosophy* 154, p. 49.

of what are effectively objective social processes. Already in the 1930s, the first generation of Frankfurt School theoreticians drew attention to how—at the very moment when global market relations began to exert their full domination, making the individual producer's success or failure dependent on market cycles totally beyond his control— the notion of a charismatic "business genius" reasserted itself in the "spontaneous capitalist ideology," attributing the success or failure of a businessman to some mysterious *je ne sais quoi* he possessed. And does not the same hold true even more so today, as the abstraction of the market relations that govern our lives is pushed to an extreme point? The bookshops are overflowing with psychological manuals advising us on how to succeed, how to outdo our partner or competitor—in short, treating success as being dependent on the proper "attitude." So, in a way, one is tempted to turn Marx's formula on its head: under contemporary capitalism, the objective market "relations between things" tend to assume the phantasmagorical form of pseudo-personalized "relations between people." And Hardt and Negri seem to fall into this trap: what they celebrate as the direct "production of life" is a structural illusion of this type.

However, before we succumb to bemoaning the "alienating" effect of the fact that "relations between persons" are replaced by "relations between things" we should nonetheless keep in mind the opposite, *liberating*, effect: the displacement of the fetishism onto "relations between things" de-fetishizes "relations between persons," allowing them to acquire "formal" freedom and autonomy. While, in a market economy, I remain *de facto* dependent, this dependency is nonetheless "civilized," enacted in the form of a "free" market exchange between me and other persons instead of in the form of direct servitude or physical coercion. It is easy to ridicule Ayn Rand, but there is a grain of truth in the famous "hymn to money" from her *Atlas Shrugged*:

Until and unless you discover that money is the root of all good, you ask for your own destruction. When money ceases to become the means by which men deal with one another, then men become the tools of other men. Blood, whips and guns or dollars. Take your choice—there is no other.[49]

Does not Marx's formula regarding how, in a commodity economy, "relations between people assume the guise of relations among things" say something similar? In the market economy, relations between people can appear as relations of mutually recognized freedom and equality: domination is no longer directly enacted or visible as such. What is problematic is Rand's underlying premise: that the only choice is between direct and indirect relations of domination and exploitation.

So what about the standard critique of "formal freedom", namely that it is in a way even worse than direct servitude, since the former is a mask that deludes one into thinking that one is free? The reply to this critical point is provided by Herbert Marcuse's old motto that "freedom is the condition of liberation": in order to demand "actual freedom," I have to have already experienced myself as basically and essentially free—only as such can I experience my actual servitude as a corruption of my human condition. In order to experience this antagonism between my freedom and the actuality of my servitude, however, I have to be recognized as formally free: the demand for my actual freedom can only arise out of my "formal" freedom. In other words, in exactly the same way as, in the development of capitalism, the formal subsumption of the production process under Capital precedes its material subsumption, formal freedom precedes actual freedom, creating the latter's conditions. The very force of abstraction which dissolves organic life-worlds is simultaneously the resource of emancipatory politics. The philosophical consequences of this real status of abstraction are crucial: they compel us to reject the historicist relativization and contextualization of different modes of subjectivity, and to assert the "abstract" Cartesian subject (*cogito*) as something

---

49 Ayn Rand, *Atlas Shrugged*, London: Penguin Books 2007, p. 871.

which today corrodes from within all different forms of cultural self-experience—no matter how far we perceive ourselves as being embedded in a particular culture, the moment we participate in global capitalism, this culture is always already de-naturalized, effectively functioning as one specific and contingent "way of life" of abstract Cartesian subjectivity.

How did we reach this new phase of the reign of abstraction? The 1968 protests focused their struggles against (what was perceived as) the three pillars of capitalism: the factory, the school, the family. As a result, each domain was subsequently submitted to postindustrial transformation: factory work is increasingly outsourced or, in the developed world at least, reorganized on a post-Fordist non-hierarchical interactive team-work basis; permanent and flexible privatized education is increasingly replacing universal public education; multiple forms of variegated sexual arrangements are replacing the traditional family.[50] The Left lost in the very moment of victory: the immediate enemy was defeated, but was replaced by a new form of even more direct capitalist domination. In "postmodern" capitalism, the market has invaded new spheres which were hitherto considered the privileged domain of the state, from education to prisons and law and order. When "immaterial work" (education, therapy, etc.) is celebrated as the kind of work which directly produces social relations, one should not forget what this means within a commodity economy: namely, that new domains, hitherto excluded from the market, are now commodified. When in trouble, we no longer talk to a friend but pay a psychiatrist or counselor to take care of the problem; children are increasingly cared for not by parents but by paid nurseries or child-minders, and so on. We are thus in the midst of a new process of the privatization of the social, of establishing new enclosures.

---

50 See Daniel Cohen, *Trois lecons sur la societe post-industrielle*, Paris: Editions du Seuil 2006.

To grasp these new forms of privatization, we need to critically transform Marx's conceptual apparatus. Because he neglected the social dimension of the "general intellect," Marx failed to envisage the possibility of *the privatization of the "general intellect" itself*—and this is what lies at the core of the struggle over "intellectual property." Negri is right on this point: within this framework, exploitation in the classical Marxist sense is no longer possible, which is why it has to be enforced more and more by direct legal measures, that is, by non-economic means. This is why, today, exploitation increasingly takes the form of rent: as Carlo Vercellone puts it, postindustrial capitalism is characterized by the "becoming-rent of the profit."[51] And this is why direct authority is needed: in order to impose the (arbitrary) legal conditions for extracting rent, conditions which are no longer "spontaneously" generated by the market. Perhaps therein resides the fundamental "contradiction" of today's "postmodern" capitalism: while its logic is de-regulatory, "anti-statal," nomadic, deterritorializing, and so on, its key tendency to the "becoming-rent-of-profit" signals a strengthening of the role of the state whose regulatory function is ever more omnipresent. Dynamic deterritorialization co-exists with, and relies on, increasingly authoritarian interventions of the state and its legal and other apparatuses. What one can discern at the horizon of our historical becoming is thus a society in which personal libertarianism and hedonism co-exist with (and are sustained by) a complex web of regulatory state mechanisms. Far from disappearing, the state is today gathering strength.

To put it another way: when, due to the crucial role of the "general intellect" (knowledge and social cooperation) in the creation of wealth, forms of wealth are increasingly "out of all proportion to the direct labour time spent on their production," the result is not, as Marx seems to have expected, the self-dissolution of capitalism, but rather the gradual relative transformation of the profit generated by the

---

51   See *Capitalismo cognitivo*, edited by Carlo Vercellone, Rome: Manifestolibri 2006.

exploitation of labor-power into rent appropriated by the privatization of this very "general intellect." Take the case of Bill Gates: how did he become the richest man in the world? His wealth has nothing to do with the cost of producing the commodities Microsoft sells (one can even argue that Microsoft pays its intellectual workers a relatively high salary). It is not the result of his producing good software at lower prices than his competitors, or of higher levels of "exploitation" of his hired workers. If this were the case, Microsoft would have gone bankrupt long ago: masses of people would have chosen programs like Linux, which are both free and, according to the specialists, better than Microsoft's. Why, then, are millions still buying Microsoft? Because Microsoft has succeeded in imposing itself as an almost universal standard, (virtually) monopolizing the field, in a kind of direct embodiment of the "general intellect." Gates became the richest man on Earth within a couple of decades by appropriating the rent received from allowing millions of intellectual workers to participate in that particular form of the "general intellect" he successfully privatized and still controls. Is it true, then, that today's intellectual workers are no longer separated from the objective conditions of their labor (they own their PC, etc.), which is Marx's description of capitalist "alienation"? Superficially, one might be tempted to answer "yes," but, more fundamentally, they remain cut off from the social field of their work, from the "general intellect," because the latter is mediated by private capital.

And the same goes for natural resources: their exploitation is one of the great sources of rent today, marked by a permanent struggle over who is to receive this rent, the peoples of the Third World or Western corporations. The supreme irony is that, in order to explain the difference between labor-power (which, when put to work, produces surplus-value over and above its own value) and other commodities (the value of which is consumed in their use and which thus involve no exploitation) Marx mentions as an example of an "ordinary" commodity *oil*, the very commodity which is today a source of extraordinary "profits." Here also, it is meaningless to link the rise and fall of oil prices to rising or falling production costs or the price of exploited labor—the production costs are negligible; the price we pay for oil is a rent we pay to the owners and controllers of this natural resource because of its scarcity and limited supply.

It is as if the three components of the production process—intellectual planning and marketing, material production, the provision of material resources—are increasingly autonomized, emerging as separate spheres. In its social consequences, this separation appears in the guise of the "three main classes" in today's developed societies, which are precisely *not* classes but three fractions of the working class: intellectual laborers, the old manual working class, and the outcasts (the unemployed, those living in slums and other interstices of public space). The working class is thus split into three, each fraction with its own "way of life" and ideology: the enlightened hedonism and liberal multiculturalism of the intellectual class; the populist fundamentalism of the old working class; more extreme and singular forms of the outcast fraction. In Hegelese, this triad is clearly the triad of the universal (intellectual workers), the particular (manual workers), and the singular (outcasts). The outcome of this process is the gradual disintegration of social life proper, of a public space in which all three fractions could meet, and "identity" politics in all its forms is a supplement for this loss. Identity politics acquires a specific form within each fraction: multicultural identity politics among the intellectual class; regressive populist fundamentalism among the working class; semi-illegal groupings (criminal gangs, religious sects, etc.) among the outcasts. What they all share is recourse to a particular identity as a substitute for the missing universal public space.

The proletariat is thus divided into three, each part being played off against the others: intellectual laborers full of cultural prejudices against "redneck" workers; workers who display a populist hatred of intellectuals and outcasts; outcasts who are antagonistic to society as such. The old cry "Proletarians, unite!" is thus more pertinent than ever: in the new conditions of "postindustrial" capitalism, the unity of the three fractions of the working class *is* already their victory. This unity, however, will not be guaranteed by any figure of the "big Other" prescribing it as the "objective tendency" of the historical process itself—the situation is thoroughly open, divided between the two versions of Hegelianism.

"We Are the Ones We Have Been Waiting For"

The future will be Hegelian—and much more radically than Fukuyama thinks. The only true alternative that awaits us—the alternative between socialism and communism—is the alternative between the two Hegels. We have already noted how Hegel's "conservative" vision uncannily points forward to "capitalism with Asian values": a capitalist civil society organized into estates and kept in check by a strong authoritarian state with managerial "public servants" and traditional values. (Contemporary Japan comes close to this model.) The choice is either this Hegel—or the Hegel of Haiti. It is as if the split into Old and Young Hegelians is to be re-enacted once again.

But what are the chances for an Hegelian Left today? Can we count only on momentary utopian explosions—like the Paris Commune, the Canudos settlement in Brazil, or the Shanghai Commune—which dissolve because of brutal external suppression or internal weaknesses, fated to remain no more than brief diversions from the main trajectory of History? Is communism then condemned to remain the utopian Idea of another possible world, an Idea whose realization necessarily ends in failure or self-destructive terror? Or should we remain heroically faithful to the Benjaminian project of the final Revolution that will redeem-through-repetition all past defeats, a day of full Reckoning? Or, more radically, should we change the field entirely, recognizing that the alternatives just proposed simply represent two sides of the same coin, that is, of the teleological-redemptive notion of history?

Perhaps the solution resides in an eschatological apocalypticism which does *not* involve the fantasy of the symbolic Last Judgment in which all past accounts will be settled; to refer to another of Benjamin's metaphors, the task is "merely" to stop the train of history which, left to its own course, leads to a precipice. (Communism is thus not the light at the end of the tunnel, that is, the happy final outcome of a long and arduous struggle—if anything, the light at the end of the tunnel is rather that of another train approaching us at full speed.) This is what a proper political act would be today: not so much to unleash a new movement, as to *interrupt* the present predominant movement. An act of "divine violence" would then mean pulling the emergency cord on the train of Historical Progress. In other words, one has to learn fully to accept that there is no big Other—or, as Badiou succinctly puts it:

> ... the simplest definition of God and of religion lies in the idea that truth and meaning are one and the same thing. The death of God is the end of the idea that posits truth and meaning as the same thing. And I would add that the death of Communism also implies the separation between meaning and truth as far as history is concerned. "The meaning of history" has two meanings: on the one hand "orientation," history goes somewhere; and then history has a meaning, which is the history of human emancipation by way of the proletariat, etc. In fact, the entire age of Communism was a period where the conviction that it was possible to take rightful political decisions existed; we were, at that moment, driven by the meaning of history. ... Then the death of Communism becomes the second death of God but in the territory of history.[52]

We should thus ruthlessly abandon the prejudice that the linear time of evolution is "on our side," that History is "working for us" like the famous old mole digging under the earth, doing the work of the Cunning of Reason. Should we then conceive of history as an open

---

52 "A conversation with Alain Badiou," *lacanian ink* 23 (2004), p. 100–1.

process in which we are offered a choice? Within this logic, history determines only the alternatives we face, the terms of the choice, but not the choice itself. At each moment of time, there are multiple possibilities waiting to be realized; once one of them is actualized, others are cancelled. The supreme case of such an agent of historical time is the Leibnizian God who created the best possible world: before creation, he had in mind the entire panoply of possible worlds, and his decision consisted in choosing the best among these options. Here, possibility precedes choice: the choice is a choice among possibilities.

Even this notion of "open" history, however, is inadequate. What is unthinkable within this horizon of linear historical evolution is the notion of a choice or act which retroactively opens up its own possibility: the idea that the emergence of the radically New retroactively changes the past—not the actual past of course (we are not in science fiction), but past possibilities (or, to put it in more formal terms, the value of modal propositions about the past). I have referred elsewhere to Jean-Pierre Dupuy's claim that, if we are to confront adequately the threat of (social or environmental) catastrophe, we need to break out of this "historical" notion of temporality: we have to introduce a new notion of time. Dupuy calls this time the "time of a project," of a closed circuit between the past and the future: the future is causally produced by our acts in the past, while the way we act is determined by our anticipation of the future and our reaction to this anticipation:

> The catastrophic event is inscribed into the future as destiny, for sure, but also as a contingent accident: it could not have taken place, even if, in *futur antérieur*, it appears as necessary. . . . if an outstanding event takes place, a catastrophe, for example, it could not not have taken place; nonetheless, insofar as it did not take place, it is not inevitable. It is thus the event's actualization—the fact that it takes place—which retroactively creates its necessity.[53]

---

53   Jean-Pierre Dupuy, *Petite metaphysique des tsunami*, Paris: Seuil 2005, p. 19.

If—accidentally—an event takes place, it creates the preceding chain which makes it appear inevitable: *this*, and not commonplaces on how underlying necessity expresses itself in and through the accidental play of appearances, is *in nuce* the Hegelian dialectic of contingency and necessity. In this sense, although we are determined by destiny, we are nonetheless *free to choose our destiny*. According to Dupuy, this is also how we should approach the ecological crisis: not to appraise "realistically" the possibilities of catastrophe, but to accept it as Destiny in the precise Hegelian sense—if the catastrophe happens, one can say that its occurrence was decided even before it took place. Destiny and free action (to block the "if") thus go hand in hand: at its most radical, freedom is the freedom to change one's Destiny.

This, then, is how Dupuy proposes to confront the disaster: we should first perceive it as our fate, as unavoidable, and then, projecting ourselves into it, adopting its standpoint, we should retroactively insert into its past (the past of the future) counterfactual possibilities ("If we had done this and that, the calamity that we are now experiencing would not have occurred!") upon which we then act today. We have to accept that, at the level of possibilities, our future is doomed, that the catastrophe will take place, that it is our destiny—and then, against the background of this acceptance, mobilize ourselves to perform the act which will change destiny itself and thereby insert a new possibility into the past. Paradoxically, the only way to prevent the disaster is to accept it as inevitable. For Badiou too, the time of the fidelity to an event is the *futur antérieur*: overtaking oneself vis-à-vis the future, one acts now as if the future one wants to bring about were already here.

What this means is that one should fearlessly rehabilitate the idea of preventive action (the "pre-emptive strike"), much abused in the "war on terror": if we postpone our action until we have full knowledge of the catastrophe, we will have acquired that knowledge only when it is too late. That is to say, the certainty on which an act relies is not a matter of knowledge, but a matter of *belief*: a true act is never a strategic intervention in a transparent situation of which we have full knowledge; on the contrary, the true act fills in the gap in our knowledge. This insight, of course, undermines the very foundations of "scientific socialism," the notion of an emancipatory process guided by scientific knowledge. Badiou recently proposed that the time has come to revoke Plato's banishment of the poets from the city and to enact a reconciliation of poetry and thought. But maybe, in view of the recent support of a number of poets for "ethnic cleansing" (viz. Radovan Karadžić), one should retain, reinforce even, Plato's misgivings about poetry, and rather endorse another break with Plato: namely, abandon his notion of philosopher-kings. One should do this not on account of the standard liberal warning about "totalitarian" Leaders who know better than ordinary people themselves what's good for them, but for a more formal reason: the reference to the big Other puts the Leader in the position of the "subject supposed to know," a subject whose activity is grounded in full knowledge (of the "laws of history," etc.)—the path is thereby open to the madness of, for example, celebrating Stalin as the greatest linguist, economist, philosopher, and so on. The moment the "big Other" falls, the Leader can no longer claim a privileged relationship to Knowledge—he becomes an idiot like everyone else.

This, perhaps, is the lesson to be learned from the traumas of the twentieth century: to keep Knowledge and the function of the Master as far apart as possible. Even the liberal notion of electing the people most "qualified" to lead is not sufficient here. One should pursue this to the end and endorse the basic insight of ancient democracy: that choice by lot is the only truly democratic choice. This is why Kojin Karatani's proposal of combining elections with lotteries in determining who will rule is more traditional than it may at first appear (he himself mentions Ancient Greece)—paradoxically, it fulfils the same function as Hegel's theory of monarchy. Karatani here takes a heroic risk in proposing a crazy-sounding definition of the difference between the dictatorship of the bourgeoisie and the dictatorship of the proletariat: "If universal suffrage by secret ballot, namely, parliamentary democracy, is the dictatorship of the bourgeoisie, the introduction of lottery should be deemed the dictatorship of the proletariat."[54]

On what can we then count? Throughout the 1950s, intellectuals who were communist fellow-travelers obeyed two axioms, one explicit, the other implicit. The first is best known in its Sartrean formulation: "an anti-Communist is a dog"; the second is that an intellectual should never, under any condition, join the Communist Party. Jean-Claude Milner characterizes this attitude as "Zenonism,"[55] referring to Zeno's paradox of Achilles and the tortoise: the fellow-traveler is Achilles with respect to the Communist Party turtle, for he is dynamic, faster, capable of overtaking the Party, and yet he always lags behind, never in fact catching up with it. With the events of 1968, this game was up: '68 took place under the sign of the "here-and-now," its protagonists wanted a revolution *now*, with no postponements—one had to either join the Party or oppose it (as the Maoists did). In other words, the '68ers wanted to unleash the pure radical activity of the masses (in this sense, the Maoist "masses who make history" are to be opposed to the passive fascist "crowds")—there is no Other, no Elsewhere, onto whom one can transfer this activity. Today, however, to be a fellow-traveler is effectively meaningless, since there is no substantial movement in relation to which one might be a fellow, no turtle inviting us to act as its Achilles.

One of the topics of 1968 that we should abandon is this misleading opposition of activity versus passivity: the idea that somehow the only truly "authentic" political stance is the one of permanent active engagement, that the primordial form of "alienation" is the passive stance which transfers activity onto the agent supposed to represent me. What lurks behind this idea is the old Leftist fascination with "direct" participatory democracy—"soviets," councils—in contrast to

54 Kojin Karatani, *Transcritique: On Kant and Marx*, Cambridge, MA: MIT Press 2003, p. 183.

55 See Jean-Claude Milner, *L'arrogance du present: Regards sur une decennie, 1965–1975*, Paris: Grasset 2009.

mere "representation"; in philosophy, it was Sartre who, in his *Critique of Dialectical Reason*, analyzed how active group-engagement becomes ossified in the *practico-inert* institutional structure. The key test of every radical emancipatory movement is, on the contrary, to what extent it transforms on a daily basis the *practico-inert* institutional practices which gain the upper hand once the fervor of the struggle is over and people return to business as usual. The success of a revolution should not be measured by the sublime awe of its ecstatic moments, but by the changes the big Event leaves at the level of the everyday, the day after the insurrection.

There is only one correct answer to those Leftist intellectuals who desperately await the arrival of a new revolutionary agent capable of instigating the long-expected radical social transformation. It takes the form of the old Hopi saying, with a wonderful Hegelian twist from substance to subject: "We are the ones we have been waiting for." (This is a version of Gandhi's motto: "Be yourself the change you want to see in the world.") Waiting for someone else to do the job for us is a way of rationalizing our inactivity. But the trap to be avoided here is that of perverse self-instrumentalization: "we are the ones we have been waiting for" does not mean we have to discover how it is we are the agent predestined by fate (historical necessity) to perform the task—it means quite the opposite, namely that there is no big Other to rely on. In contrast to classical Marxism where "history is on our side" (the proletariat fulfils the predestined task of universal emancipation), in the contemporary constellation, the big Other is *against* us: left to itself, the inner thrust of our historical development leads to catastrophe, to apocalypse; what alone can prevent such calamity is, then, *pure voluntarism*, in other words, our free decision to act against historical necessity. In a way, the Bolsheviks found themselves in a similar predicament at the end of the civil war in 1921: two years before his death, when it became clear that there would be no imminent European-wide revolution and that the idea of building socialism in one country was nonsense, Lenin wrote:

What if the complete hopelessness of the situation, by stimulating the efforts of the workers and peasants tenfold, offered us the opportunity to create the fundamental requisites of civilization in a different way from that of the West European countries?[56]

Is this not the predicament of the Morales government in Bolivia, of the former Aristide government in Haiti, and of the Maoist government in Nepal? They came to power through "fair" democratic elections, not through insurrection, but once in power, they exerted it in a way which was (partially, at least) "non-statal": directly mobilizing their grassroots supporters and bypassing the party–state representative network. Their situation is "objectively" hopeless: the whole drift of history is basically against them, they cannot rely on "objective tendencies," all they can do is to improvise, do what they can in a desperate situation. Nevertheless, does this not give them a unique freedom? One is tempted to apply here the old distinction between "freedom from" and "freedom for": does their freedom from History (with its laws and objective tendencies) not sustain their freedom for creative experimentation? In their activity, they can rely only on the collective will of their supporters.

We can count on unexpected allies in this struggle. The fate of Victor Kravchenko—the Soviet diplomat who, in 1944, defected while in New York and then wrote his famous bestselling memoir, *I Chose Freedom*—is worth mentioning here.[57] His book was the first substantial first-person report on the horrors of Stalinism, beginning with a detailed account of forced collectivization and mass hunger in Ukraine, where Kravchenko himself—in the early 1930s still a true believer in the system—participated in enforcing collectivization. The more widely known story about him ends in 1949, when he triumphed in a major trial against his Soviet accusers in Paris, who had even brought his ex-wife to court to testify to his corruption, alcoholism,

---

56   V.I. Lenin, *Collected Works*, Vol. 33, Moscow: Progress Publishers 1966, p. 479.
57   See Mark Jonathan Harris's outstanding documentary on Kravchenko, *The Defector* (2008).

and record of domestic violence. What is much less well known is that, immediately after this victory, while he was being hailed all around the world as a Cold War hero, Kravchenko became deeply worried about the McCarthyite anti-communist witch-hunt, and warned that in using such methods to fight Stalinism the US only risked becoming more like its opponent. He also become increasingly aware of the injustices of the liberal democracies, and his desire to see changes in Western society developed almost into an obsession. After writing a much less popular sequel to his *I Chose Freedom*, significantly entitled *I Chose Justice*, Kravchenko set out on a crusade to find a new, less exploitative, mode of organizing production. This led him to Bolivia, where he ploughed his money into organizing poor farmers into new collectives. Crushed by the failure of these endeavors, he withdrew into solitude and eventually shot himself at his home in New York. His suicide was the consequence of his despair, not the result of some KGB blackmail—proof that his denunciation of the Soviet Union had been a genuine act of protest against injustice.

Today, new Kravchenkos are emerging everywhere, from the US to India, China and Japan, from Latin America to Africa, the Middle East to Western and Eastern Europe. They are disparate and speak different languages, but they are not as few as may appear—and the greatest fear of the rulers is that these voices will start to reverberate and reinforce each other in solidarity. Aware that the odds are pulling us towards catastrophe, these actors are ready to act against all odds. Disappointed by twentieth-century Communism, they are ready to "begin from the beginning" and reinvent it on a new basis. Decried by enemies as dangerous utopians, they are the only people who have really awakened from the utopian dream which holds most of us under its sway. They, not those nostalgics for twentieth-century "Really Existing Socialism," are our only hope.

The fact that Deleuze, just before he died, was in the middle of writing a book on Marx, is indicative of a wider trend. In the Christian past, it was common for people who had led dissolute lives to return to the safe haven of the church in old age, so they might die reconciled with God. Something similar is happening today with many anti-communist Leftists. In their final years, they return to communism as if, after their life of depraved betrayal, they want to die reconciled with the communist Idea. As with the old Christians, these late conversions carry the same basic message: that we have spent our lives rebelling vainly against what, deep within us, we knew all the time to be the truth. So, when even a great anti-communist like Kravchenko can in a certain sense return to his faith, our message today should be: do not be afraid, join us, come back! You've had your anti-communist fun, and you are pardoned for it—time to get serious once again!